LASTING IMPACT

NAVIGATING THE RIPPLING EFFECTS OF SUICIDE

EDWARD V. AGUILAR

FINN-PHYLLIS
PRESS

Copyright © 2019 by Edward V. Aguilar.

Published by Finn-Phyllis Press, Inc.

All Rights Reserved. Printed in the United States of America. This book may not be reproduced in whole or in part, in any form or by any means, electronic or mechanical, including photocopying, recording, or by any information storage and retrieval system now known or hereafter invented, without the express written permission of the author.

Lasting Impact / Edward V. Aguilar - 1st ed.

ISBN 978-0-9998670-6-8 (pbk)

ISBN 978-0-9998670-7-5 (eBook)

Book Cover design by JetLaunch.net

www.MindsetMtn.com

DEDICATION

To my mother, Martha, your guidance to explore what this world has to offer reignited me. You've been an example of continuing to live a fulfilled existence no matter what life brings our way.

To my father, Richard, rest in peace. Without your guidance both to lead and to be a student when necessary, I'd be lost in my attempts to create impact in this world.

You both serve as my lighthouse as I navigate toward my own shore in order to leave a positive, lasting impact upon this world.

FOREWORD

Several years back, I hosted a webinar. I don't remember the exact reason for doing so, but the topic was tying personal development to the concepts of depression, self-doubt, and—at a high level—suicide.

When I posted an announcement on Facebook for the webinar, a friend of my girlfriend commented.

"What are your credentials?" she asked. "What is your background that gives you the ability to speak on this topic of suicide?"

Here we go, I thought to myself. *Do I really have the credentials to be openly discussing this topic?*

"Well," I responded, knowing that others would see the banter about to take place, "if you're looking for me to have some piece of paper that qualifies me to speak on this topic, I have no degree to speak of. I do, however, know what it's like to sit in a room with a 12-gauge in my mouth and my finger on the trigger, if that helps. Also, I lost a cousin to suicide as well as four or five friends I grew up with. I've also lost co-workers and friends I met later in my life. Finally, I've helped several individuals so that they didn't follow through with their plan to take their own lives."

I anxiously anticipated her response.

"Good!" she said. "I'm tired of hearing about homelessness from someone who has never been homeless but has studied it. I don't want to hear about suicide from someone who has never dealt with any aspect of suicide in their personal life."

My "credentials" to speak on the topic were officially being questioned, and it was a moment I'd anticipated for some time. I've questioned my credentials *myself* from time to time. The truth is, we all question our credentials at different times in our lives and for different reasons.

In addition to the credentials I've just referenced, I'm a small town boy from Williams, Arizona (more commonly referred to as The Gateway to the Grand Canyon). I have held and hold many titles: son, grandson, nephew, cousin, uncle, friend, dad, coach, student, teacher, man, boy, connector, and athlete. The list will continue to include titles such as business owner, author, full-time speaker and—one day I hope—grandfather. I'm the father of a young lady I began raising when she was just a year and a half old. She recently graduated from high school. I am also the father of a young man who is entering his sophomore year in high school; before I know it, he will be out on his own as well.

Perhaps you're wondering, "Was it really necessary to list off *all* of those titles, Eddie?" I get it. I asked myself the same question. And the more I thought about it, I realized that it was indeed necessary, if for no other reason, because we forget who we are at times.

A question that has swirled around in my head and heart many times over the past several years is, "Why am I trying to write this book?" I mean, hell, it's long overdue, and I've run my mouth a multitude of times about it nearing completion. The truth is, every time I begin to walk away from it for one reason or another, I'm drawn back into the topic many fear to speak on, let alone think about. The word "suicide" is a hell of a word with a frightening intensity. It holds great power over many lives, including mine. I've long felt the need to write this book, and as you read *my* truths when it comes to this dark topic, perhaps they will shed some much-needed light on it. The key is that these are *my* truths, and I own them as such.

I once had the opportunity to interview a passionate author and podcaster by the name of Adam Lowery. I highly recommend his book and podcast, both titled *The Cognitive Rampage*, to those interested in further exploring the topic of mental health. Adam often poses a great question: "If you ride a roller coaster and tell me it was the most fun ride ever created, and I ride the same roller coaster and tell you it was the scariest ride man has ever created, *who is right?*"

It's all about perspective. The truth about who is right and who is wrong is rarely set in stone. For you, the roller coaster was the most fun ride you've ever been on. For me, the hell if I'm ever getting back onto it! This book is intended to give you the perspective of *my* truth based off of *my* experiences and who *I* am. You may vibe with some of what I say, and you may work hard to negate my perspective based upon *your* truths and who *you* are. That's fine; it's also to be expected. For those of you who might feel compelled to completely tear down any of my points, please remember the roller coaster.

As we wade into the topic of suicide, allow me to use this concept of perspective as an example of how best to absorb the information to come. You may have been impacted by the loss of a loved one to suicide, or perhaps you have considered closing the book to your own story too soon. Regardless of the position you're in, when you read the above paragraph about my goal of sharing *my* truth and *my* perspective, did you receive it as a bit standoffish, as a way for me to protect myself from the judgements and feelings of other? Maybe you did. And maybe you didn't. All I know is that I've started this conversation that same way before for the same reasons I am now: is the act of suicide right or wrong? My answer is that, just like you, I'm a human being trying to figure out this thing called life. The only tool I can do that with is my own truth and perspective at any point in time.

What I most want you to come to understand about suicide and its lasting impact—even if you're deeply considering taking this action yourself—is that the truth is, there is not one person on the face of this planet who has the ultimate answer in terms of whether it is right or wrong. There is not one person who has been given the authority to declare whether or not suicide is selfish. There is not one person who holds the magical card that presents simple solutions to overcoming a suicide or suicide attempt, or simple solutions that would easily prevent one from taking his own life. There is no person who can tell you for sure whether or not your pain is real.

Remember the roller coaster.

I've sat with a gun in my mouth, overwhelmingly depressed. I've also sat—many times over—with a mother who held onto endless guilt for her son's suicide. He was one of my best friends, and she held onto the guilt for his choice for years. I had a man my age message me on Facebook, thanking me for having saved his life through a video I recorded years prior—only to attend his funeral within two years of receiving that message. He decided to take his life without again reaching out to me.

For whatever reason, God has placed me in a position to encounter a high number of suicides or suicide survivors. A guy I fought forest fires with as a Hotshot took his girlfriend's life, her son's life, and then his own life. A friend who got married and then became a widow had her life taken *by* her next husband as she laid in her bed while her three girls slept in the other room. Those girls heard a second shot as he took his own life. To top it off, the daughter she adopted before her husband passed away from cancer had already lost her own mother at a young age to suicide. I could never fathom this reality: losing my mother to suicide and my dad to cancer, being adopted by my stepmom, and then having her murdered as I slept in the next room. While these stories might help put things into perspective for you, they are not relayed as an attempt to take away or even lessen your pain. Whatever pain you may feel is true to you in this moment, and it's valid.

Conceptually, the act of a suicide is no different from the reasons society doesn't face the topic head on. We are told to sweep our shit under the rug, and we are encouraged to sweep the topic under the rug while hoping we are never personally affected by it. Suicide is a taboo subject that's continuously avoided. The word itself causes many to cringe. It is my hope that this book will acknowledge this fact and persuade others to discuss the topic, even just in small circles.

I'd like to ask you to consider something. I know I'm asking you to emotionally commit yourself, given that you've been impacted by suicide either through having a friend or loved one who's considered or died from suicide, or you have considered it for yourself. Even if you're diving into the topic out of mere curiosity, the question is an important one to consider. Have you ever heard about a suicide and thought, "That didn't surprise me"? I'll give you one that stumped the world: Robin Williams. As I've gone through the many names of those I've known who committed suicide, the majority of them are individuals I never would have expected to do such a thing. We so often wonder why that is so.

It's important to return to the fact that both the word and the act have a stigma associated with them. Suicide is the elephant in the room we do our best to ignore. But let me ask you about your thoughts when it comes to suicide as a general topic, or the last time you learned that someone you knew personally or through other means had committed suicide. Please be honest with your immediate thoughts and responses.

If you're not, you're simply glossing over it in order to try to make sense of it (despite your initial reaction).

Many speak about the selfishness of a suicide. I understand their perspective, but remember that there is a backstory to *everyone's* backstory, as there is a backstory to *your* backstory. The reality is this: one sweeps his or her problems and issues under the rug just as you, those around you, and society choose to sweep this very topic under the rug. Competing for space in one's mind and heart during dark times are issues, challenges, emotions, and confusion over what's right and wrong. Many have professed, "We just need more 'suicide awareness.'" The truth is, many of us are aware. We are *extremely* aware, and it's time that suicide becomes a more openly talked about issue. So many are suffering who don't realize that they *aren't* alone—they're simply trapped in the darkness that consumes their world.

When one is struggling, he or she needs to learn how to fearlessly scream for help. We live in a world where a "home run" has higher value than hitting continuous singles. We live in a world where a slam dunk has higher value than a shot banked off of the backboard—even though they're both worth the same two points. When battling depression, openly facing the social stigma and creating alternative ways to battle the darkness is more simple than you might believe. Yet, not having viable solutions isn't the problem. Today's societal values toward and the tendency to minimize suicide are demolishing the lives of individuals and families alike.

Are there ways to move through the pits we fall into in life? Are there ways to overcome the darkness? Are those battling doing so alone while feeling shame, guilt, and fear of losing their battle by taking their own lives? Is a good life available to us after the suicide of a loved one? The list of questions I frequently hear goes on, and will continue to grow unless we provide solutions and solution-focused actions for others to take.

I pray that this book will provide guidance, clarity, or even a minimal basis for understanding the lasting impact suicide has on the world. I pray that it will be impactful in the ways that those who have graciously provided testimonies hoped it would in order to save just one life. If just one life is saved, this book will have more than served its purpose.

ONE

Summer of 2004 through Father's Day of 2005 will always be the darkest time of my life. Originally from Arizona, I had moved with my wife and kids from Las Vegas to Illinois.

I had the mentality of being the "man of the family" and was willing to move across the country to the area where my ex-wife grew up. Shit, I was Eddie Aguilar, an ex-hotshot of 10 years who, at times, led an elite wildfire suppression crew into the woods, mountains, or even deserts of the U.S. under extreme circumstances. To move across the country with my family and create a life for all of us would, therefore, be simple. Wouldn't it? Little did I know, life would not go as planned.

Having struggled to find work combined with having a mortgage that was tough as hell to pay, I found myself in a dark place six to seven months after we arrived in Illinois. I felt like my life had come crashing down upon me. I'd never felt so alone.

To this day, I have always felt that God has had His hand placed upon my shoulder, especially when I needed it the most. You'll come to understand far more deeply as you continue through these pages the experiences through which I came to believe this. Little did I know during one particular week that I'd come to a set of crossroads and was placed in a position that would have changed the trajectory of the many lives had the outcome been different.

The imperfections of the cold steel so clearly live in my mind. The bead that hunters know all too well—the one that rests upon the tip of a 12-gauge shotgun—had been sawed off the Remington 870 Wingmaster. I hadn't intentionally converted it to a sawed-off shotgun. The barrel had become packed with mud during a duck hunt several years prior, and had subsequently mushroomed. Thank God the next shot I took during that hunt didn't explode the barrel in a way that would've harmed me.

I woke up one Sunday morning in a funk due to some events that had occurred in my personal life several days prior. There was major static between myself and my then-wife. I was pissed and upset, lost and frustrated, trying to provide for my family. I was failing, and my wife and I were distant in so many ways. I had to get out of the house, so I left for work early just to try to keep my sanity. At that time, I was working at a Cingular Wireless kiosk in the mall.

"Is that a Bible up there?" I heard a young man ask as he walked up to my desk and pointed at the cabinet behind me.

Turning around in my chair as I sat at my desk, I asked, "What are you talking about?"

"Up there, on top of the cabinet" he pointed, as I swiveled back around to see where he was looking.

"Oh no," I said, finally seeing what he was referring to. "That's my planner. God knows right now I need to be diving into The Bible though."

This young man then said, "If it wasn't for God, I'd be dead or in prison. God saved my life. I had several friends who've been murdered, are hooked on drugs, or are in prison."

"Yeah, I have a friend going through some shit right now," I continued. When we first met, he was on God's path and was doing great. He had spent several years in prison before we met, but when we met he was sober and doing well. Now he's strayed, and I'm worried he'll be dead or in prison soon, just like some of your boys."

For some reason, I was sharing the fact that my friend, Robert, had been on my mind.

After my computer booted up, I looked up this young man's account in our system. "Man, I can't find your number or information," I said.

Just then, my cell phone began ringing.

"Oh shoot," the young man said, "I'm not with you guys. I'm with that company right there," he said, pointing to the kiosk next to ours. "As for your friend, he'll find his way back to God. I'll pray for him, brother." He then walked away.

As the phone continued to ring, I looked down to see who was calling. "That's strange," I thought. It was our family friend, George, and I'd just been speaking about his son, Robert, to this stranger who was "accidentally" at the wrong kiosk.

"Hey, George. What's going on? How are you doing?" I asked.

"Not good Eddie," he replied. I felt my heart sink. "Robert would've wanted me to call you."

What the fuck does he mean, "Robert would've wanted me to call you"? I thought.

"Eddie," I heard him say weakly, the wind still obviously knocked out of him, "Robert shot himself yesterday, and he's not going to make it. He's been on life support all night, and this morning, we're going to take him off so we can donate his organs."

"What? When? How? Why?" All these questions ran through my head simultaneously. I knew not to ask them, that in that moment the answers didn't matter. There is a time and place for those kinds of common questions after a death, and this moment wasn't it. Sometimes it feels as if knowing the answers might alleviate the jolt of emotional pain we've encountered as our human nature tries to rationalize something we consider irrational.

"I'm so sorry, George! I have no idea what to say; I'm at a loss." I was clueless as to how to respond, given the shit going on in my own world. "Poor Suzanne," I replied, thinking about Robert's mother. "I know this is going to kill her."

"She's been with him all night." He said. "I tried to keep her from seeing him like this, but you know her, she wouldn't have it. Eddie, you were important to Robert. I wanted you to hear it from me before hearing from anybody else and before we take him off the machines."

"I don't know what to say, George. I'm sorry," I consoled. "I will pray for you two and talk to you guys soon. Please give Suzanne a hug for me. And George...I'm sorry."

After hanging up, the young man with whom I'd spoken a few minutes earlier walked by again.

"Hey," I called to grab his attention. "You know my buddy I was just talking about?" I asked.

"Yeah," he responded, almost as though he knew something was up.

"When you were leaving and my phone began ringing, it was his dad calling," I shared. His eyes grew wide. "He shot himself last night, and this morning they are taking him off the machines and letting him go." His look said it all; a stranger he'd just met spoke of a friend he was worried about, and now he knew why.

"Oh, man...I'm sorry! I'll pray for him and you," he said. "Don't worry man, God will get a hold of him." I was then once again alone in my world in some desolate mall in Bloomingdale, Illinois, distant from anybody and anything I've ever known.

Fuckin' Robert, I knew something was going on. Why the hell didn't you answer my calls or texts? I sat there with my thoughts, wondering in what specific moment he decided to leave this world. When would be the exact time that he would pass on? Had it already happened? Who do I reach out to about this? It was a cold winter on the outskirts of Chicago, as people looking to avoid the winter's brisk chill walked past the stores to get their day's morning walk in. The cold breeze from the lake had now entered my heart and any sense of warmth that was left there grew distant.

Robert was the seventh or eighth person I'd known who had chosen to take their life, but this time was different. As I was dealing with my own shit, Robert had been my focus. I believed that if I could only help him get through his shit, maybe I'd find some resolution in my own life, which was quickly spiraling into dark depths. I'd call him during my long drives to a job that provided no satisfaction; sometimes he'd answer, and other times he wouldn't. I knew deep down that he was spiraling just as I was. His mom and dad were nearby, as was his beautiful daughter, so he even had some sort of connection--the kind of connection I felt like I didn't have during this time. Robert was 37 years old when he left this world.

I flashed back to the day Robert's daughter, Kelsey Morgan, was born. We were tending to a wildfire south of Grants, New Mexico, when we got the call on our radios. "Robert, you're about to be a dad, and you need to get back to Flagstaff. Eddie why don't you take him." These words brought excitement to the whole crew.

This dude from SD, as he always referred to his hometown of San Diego, was a strong individual. He'd made mistakes in life and he'd paid his dues. His life was finally where he wanted it to be. As a husband, a son with loving parents, and a soon-to-be father, to see his nerves get the better of him was exciting. I was blessed to be given the gift of chaperoning him as we hauled ass toward Grants, then hit I-40 and headed west to tie in with his dad somewhere on the highway.

We spoke of the change that was about to rock his world, a beautiful baby girl whom he would soon father. Not only was he nervous about becoming a father, he was hoping to make it back to Flagstaff in time to be with his wife as their daughter was born.

Excitedly, we met George at an exit that hosted the usual tourist traps, selling mementos to people traveling east or west on the long stretch of Interstate 40. Off they sped as one man was about to become a father, and the elder man—who had come into his life and taken on the role as *his* father—was about to become a grandfather.

As the memory faded from my mind, I sat alone in the mall that brought me nothing but disappointment. I was filled with many emotions. Anger toward Robert hit me hard; I was pissed that he didn't reach out to me. I also felt as though he deserted me, leaving me to be alone with the shit I was going through.

"Who the fuck do I call now?" I whispered to myself, remembering how I typically called him on my drive home to vent about the unhappiness in my life.

My emotions then took a turn toward George, the man who took on the responsibility of fathering Robert later on in his life. This man who Robert called "Dad" was losing a son, and he was about to go on a long journey with his wife, as she was about to lose her only child.

My heart sank even deeper as I thought about Robert's mom, Suzanne. "This is going to kill her," I thought to myself, knowing that she loved her son like no other person on the planet. He was her pride and joy, and he was finally becoming the man she had known he could become despite his self-inflicted setbacks in life.

It's a good thing she's young and won't know what's going on right now, I thought to myself, as Kelsey Morgan came to mind. Not that there is ever a good time to lose someone, but I knew that losing someone in this way and not being able to comprehend why he'd take his own life would haunt her one day.

The workday began, and customers began entering the Stratford Square Mall. My co-worker (who would later become my supervisor) had come in, and I shared the news with her. She recommended that I go home, but I wanted to stay away from home for as long as possible. That's horrible, isn't it? That the one place that should bring the most comfort and safety is the furthest of places to which one wants to go?

As my workday finally ended, I drove north and headed home. *I need to call someone*, I thought, reaching for my phone. Instinct and habit caused me to pull up Robert's number. My heart stopped, realizing my brother would never again answer any of my calls. *Shit*, I thought, *This is real. You fucker, who do I have to talk to now?* I silently asked Robert once again.

Once I got home, my wife knew something was up. First of all, I was pissed at her because of what had been going on between us. I had moved all the way to Chicago, distant from family and friends in a world that was foreign to me, and I felt lost. My marriage was crumbling. I wasn't bringing in enough money. I had no one to talk to or reach out to locally for help. And now, I'd lost a good friend who chose to leave this world on his own.

The walls were caving in.

"What's wrong?" she asked.

"I had a friend pass today. He killed himself."

To be honest, I don't remember the rest of the conversation that night, but I wasn't going to tell her that the friend who passed was Robert due to a prior conversation we had about him that didn't go terribly well.

The next 24 hours remain a blur up until the point when I was so exhausted and upset that I chose to lay down on the floor in our bedroom and pass out. I felt my body finally begin to give in and my mind begin to rest. I was half asleep when I was jolted awake in a way I never had been before.

I jumped up off the floor and burst into tears, bawling my ass off. I ran downstairs, as what had just happened scared me in a way I've never before been scared. "What the fuck was that about?" I screamed.

What happened was, when I was almost into a deep sleep, I

had a feeling that frightened me. I felt the concussion from the muzzle blast of an imaginary gun to the side of my head. I still know that feeling to this moment, as it's awakened me on more than one occasion. The muzzle blast from a gun had made its presence known to me, and the worst part of it was that it felt far too real. After running downstairs dripping with tears, my wife followed me to see what was going on.

"I felt the blast of the gun! I felt it against my head," I stuttered, still crying harder than ever.

"What the hell?" she asked. "What's going on? Who was it that killed himself?"

I fought back the urge to tell her; I felt as though she didn't deserve to know who I had just lost. Finally, I shot back at her after she asked several times: "Robert killed himself."

Her eyes grew wide, and she got pissed. "How come you didn't tell me it was Robert?" she shot back, upset that I didn't let her know it was someone she knew.

"What the fuck does it matter to you?" I asked.

The rest of the night was a blur as I tried to sleep on the couch but was unable to, continuing to fear the feeling that woke me earlier. What caused that feeling? Where did it come from? Was I losing my mind? Where was I supposed to go from there?

As a kid, I lay awake in bed many nights shaking and scared after my dad had his share of alcohol for the night and was vocally aggressive with my mom. I hated it, so I'd hit or kick the wall in order to let them know I was awake. Then, one of them would come pull me out of the room. My dad struggled with the aftermath of coming back from the Vietnam War, having been shot. 'Nam impacted him pretty hard, and I got to see the aftermath of war as a child. Due to his aggressive nature within his marriage, I went to the opposite extreme in my own. This didn't serve me or the marriage at all.

For the next few days, I worked and moped, and by the weekend, Robert had left this world and the thin strand of rope

I was hanging onto began slipping from my grasp. I was lost. I was hurting. I was in a place I thought I'd never end up, especially after previously seeing the rippling effects of suicide. My wife and I had another disagreement. This one, however, was different; it triggered many new thoughts and emotions and exposed my truest feelings at that point in time.

After arguing about God knows what, I said the words I never thought I'd hear myself say: "Maybe Robert made the right decision," implying that taking one's life is an acceptable solution. My wife knew exactly what I meant. Her instinct, and rightfully so, was to get out of the house and take my son with her, as my daughter was already away for the night. Never did I consider hurting her or my children, but the smart thing for her to do was to take my son out of the situation.

After she left, I consumed whatever alcohol we had, which wasn't much given our lack of money for beer or whiskey. I then sat alone with my thoughts. I felt Robert's pain as I contemplated what I was going to do and how I was going to do it.

I felt completely lost with nowhere to turn. I was hurt, feeling a pain I thought would never go away. Remember the titles I spoke of earlier? Father, son, grandson, friend, cousin, nephew... None of them entered my thoughts in that moment. I was lost in the wilderness of my mind without a single feeling resembling comfort or peace. My blood became chilled by the cold that surrounded my life. Not even a smile from my children could warm me with hope for a better tomorrow (nor was it their job to provide that for me).

I believed it was time for me to relieve this world of the burden I'd become. I went into the master bedroom upstairs and sat on the end of the bed. I clicked the safety button off, placed the butt of the 12-gauge on the floor between my legs, placed the cold steel barrel into my mouth, and rested a finger on the trigger.

Where the fuck did this all begin? I thought to myself.

As I sat in that pit of darkness, the saddest part is what I *didn't* think about!

I didn't think about my son.

I didn't think about my daughter.

Or my mom.

Or my dad.

Or my uncles, aunts, and cousins.

Or my brothers.

I didn't think about anybody except myself and the pain that I had felt, not just for the prior week but for a long, long time.

Now I had a new challenge that would test who I was as a man: Was I "man enough" to follow through with taking my own life, or would I be a screw-up at that as well?

As I had already done many times over already (though it had been a while since the last time), I was able to flip the mental switch that would give me the determination to follow through. I became focused, and was definitely ready to get this done by blocking the hurt and pain for long enough to apply full pressure to the arched trigger of the shotgun as it sat secured between my feet, the barrel inserted into my mouth.

Slowly, I began to apply pressure, knowing there was a slight distance between the point of applying pressure and the point where the trigger would do just that—trigger a chain of events that would alter the lives of many, while hopefully ending mine.

Knowing I was close to the point of no return, I prayed that I finished the job and would not survive what was about to happen. So sad, but definitely true. The trigger was tense, and there was a break in the silence. For whatever reason, while I was slowly applying pressure, I wasn't resisting. My crying was no longer audible. All signs that anything physically existing in my world ceased to exist.

Then came the voice.

"I just left my daughter behind, and now you mean to tell

me you're going to leave your kids behind?" The question was clear and concise.

I immediately shoved the Remington away from me and released a child-like cry.

WHAT THE HELL JUST HAPPENED?

A wave of emotions overcame me, and I sobbed like a two-year-old who lost his favorite blanket. I was really going to go through with this, wasn't I? At that moment, I recognized the strength of power my mind had once it was committed to doing something, and the only stop to this particular action was this intervention.

The voice I heard was Robert's.

My boy from SD spoke to me, and he called me out on my shit! Why didn't I didn't see the lasting impact of *his* suicide and realize that I was about to cause the same to my two kids? Not only that, my death would've likely impacted my mother the same way his had impacted Suzanne.

I was still lost. But I knew that, with time, I could regain my direction.

I was hurt. But I knew that time would heal my wounds if I allowed myself to receive such a blessing.

I was still scared. But I knew that there were people in this world who carried a strength that they could shed upon me until I regained my own.

Most important, I knew the example I would have set for my children had I taken my life. I know for a fact that the likelihood of them following through with such an act, had I done so, would have increased many times over. Knowing this still makes me cringe at times.

You see, when we are caught up in the darkness, as I was, the world outside of our internal selves becomes non-existent. As I said before, the innocence and spirit of my young children couldn't shed even a drop of light upon my heart and soul, and to this day that fact saddens me if I allow it to. From that day forward, I've never again thought of allowing myself to return to such a place of darkness.

Having experienced the impacts of suicide many times over has, in a sense, numbed me to it all—until I began writing about it, that is.

You might be asking yourself a multitude of questions:

"How do I overcome thoughts of suicide?"

"How do I overcome the loss of a loved one to suicide?"

"Am I alone in my situation?"

"Am I alone in my thoughts?"

"Is there light following the darkness?"

Many additional questions might be floating through your mind as well. The truth is, suicide is a tough topic to bring out into the open and discuss.

Several years back, I told my story to an organization here in Northern Arizona called NACA (Native Americans for Community Action). My mom and grandmother were helping to serve food, and my son and daughter were present as well. My daughter knew that I'd almost taken my life, but my son, who was 10 at the time, knew nothing of the experience.

"Hey Bubs, I have something to tell you," I began, as I pulled him aside before I was to speak. "I'm going to speak on something that might make you sad, but you need to understand why I'm doing this."

He looked at me intently. "I'm going to be speaking about suicide, and I know you don't know, but when you were two years old and we lived in Illinois, I almost took my own life."

Tears began seeping from the corner of his eyes, and I reached up to wipe them away.

"But can I tell you why I didn't, nor have I considered, nor *will* I consider it ever again?" I asked.

He nodded.

"Because of you and your sister. Because of you, I never will do that, and by sharing my story with these people here, hopefully God will help me help one person who might be hurting. Okay?"

He smiled, knowing that he would be half of the reason that, from that point forward, no matter how bad life got, I would never take my own life.

After sharing my story with the audience, a lady in her mid-thirties approached me. "I want to thank you for sharing your story with all of us. For many years, I took on the blame after my brother drank himself to death. I've always felt it was my fault, and I lived in guilt because of it. Now I know it wasn't my fault. Thank You!" She then walked off, not even giving me time to reply. My son was a witness to this—to the power of one's story.

Through the darkness, light can be found.

What if overcoming your obstacle today is positioning you to someday be a blessing to someone else down the road?

Allow your "what ifs" to be positive in nature, not questions that result in a negative ending.

Let the journey begin!

TWO

This is a piece I wrote after reflecting upon the toughest time of my life. It's a story I wrote while thinking about Robert's last days as well as the day on which I, too, almost became a statistic. It was inspired by a counseling session I had with a pastor who told me I was too focused on what was in the palm of my hand, never looking up from the focus of what laid in my palm.

Sitting in Silence

Sitting in silence, my eyes have opened. My focus has not altered its direction the slightest bit as the coolness resides in my palm. Rolling from right to left, then back again, my focus remains as the motions continue. Remembrance of its beginning, as this thing was once the size of a marble, and now this ball of steel has continued to grow and consume my thoughts. From its beginnings as a grain of sand, its current touch now chills my veins as my blood's temperature resembles that of a winter's runoff.

At times I've felt a warmth upon my shoulder emitting an energy that I shoo away as it attempts to turn me away from my focus. I will not dare to turn away. I cannot. This ball is my life, which I have to conquer. Until it diminishes, until the warm winds carry its remains from my palm, my purpose in life will not be resolved.

All that I am begins to fade. As each day passes, the breeze slowly takes away what I value, and the passion in my heart tends to slowly dissipate. At times, I shift my focus for brief moments, viewing flashes of light as warm wisps of air brush against my cheek. Soft whispers of tender voices ease my soul. My energy then returns to what lies in my palm.

I can't lose focus.

The number of days increasingly pass as I begin to notice I am less in the presence of others. That which resides in my palm still continues to grow from day to day, its chill flowing through my body, diminishing any feelings of comfort I've come to know. Glimpses of light present themselves less and less often. I have grown weaker. My soul aches to be touched, but I cannot defer my attention. From within, I grasp for every ounce of strength in an effort to crumble into powder what one hand can no longer embrace.

I now find myself standing alone. My shoulders hunch, as what I now hold requires both of my hands to embrace. I close my eyes and bow my head to reflect. In doing so, the rain begins to pour as the skies darken. The water from above transforms itself into splinters, forcefully inserting themselves deep within my body, into what remains of my soul. Thunder cracks like a whip, teasing my senses, as if I am about to be persecuted for who I've become.

What is this I hold?

What lies within my palms which I've refused to let go?

Why am I alone, tending to myself? Where did my loved ones go?

I am not afraid to die. Though never had I envisioned the end feeling so dark and cold. I am a shell of what I have been. My existence is no longer worthy. What resides in so much weight that I've chosen never to release?

My fears live within that of which I'm unable to let go. My frights and disappointments add to its density. My mistakes and hurts blend into the makeup of my focus.

That which has consumed me lays my burdens. To come this far, I have nothing but shame. I cannot journey back, for I feel the pain will be worse than that which has brought me to this point. I could never fathom returning to where I once was. My purpose, whatever it may have been, no longer resides within.

So here I stand. My eyes have opened, at the edge of a boardwalk, which has led me to the deepest of the darkest seas. This, I realize, is my time. I take one last look around, only to find myself in solitude. This weight I hold shall sink with me to the depths of darkness.

Because I stand alone, I will not be missed.

My eyes begin to trickle beads of tears upon my face. I begin to weep as a child having lost its mother, and I'm now standing in darkness. I let my emotions explode as I have never done before. In one last request, to which or whom I speak, I have no understanding. I choose to ask for forgiveness.

Forgiveness for not having a purpose.

Forgiveness for allowing myself to become what I have become.

Forgiveness for not loving anymore.

Forgiveness for any hurt I've caused those who love me.
Forgiveness for the hurt toward innocent ones, whom I've never come to fully know.
Forgiveness for not having a fear to die.
And in one last explosion, I ask for forgiveness of having a fear to live!
It's too late to turn back. The time has come, and I stand at the edge as the rains drench me. The thunder vibrates in rhythm so as to give me a countdown to my destruction. I close my eyes one last time as tears flood my cheeks. The countdown has begun.
Three...Two...One.
Action has finally taken place. My senses allow me to feel the chilling waters. My eardrums echo from the thunderous splash of the weight entering the sea. The water numbs my face as the icy liquid engulfs me for a split second.
Now, with eyes wide open, the sting becomes less and less, as I find myself standing in solitude. My hands are free as the rains ricochet and begin to fill the cups of my palms with healing waters. What the hell happened; did I just choose to let go?
Why did I not sink with what had burdened me for so long? I try not to question my actions, but what the hell happened? I begin feeling anxiety once again, but nothing like it was. Immediately, I feel as though I need an answer to what just happened. What exactly brought me to this point of fear, pain, and hurt?
"Can't things just be?" I heard a soft voice whisper into my ear. It was then that I relived those intense moments I'd just encountered.
There was a grasp upon my right shoulder, which I felt allowing me to let go of the heavy weight. It was a familiar touch, but I still had no idea where it came

from. This same grasp intensified as a warm sensation overrode the freezing temperature in my heart. The tears that flowed down my face began warming my cheeks.

For once in a long time, I know I am no longer alone. Pain still resides in my heart, but as I exhale, I am able to inhale without struggle. The sensation of my tears begins to melt the ice from within. Upon my lips, my tears are no longer bitter but instead resemble sweetness from the fruits of life. My senses have given me hope. The grasp still remains upon my shoulder. Still feeling this, I am taken back to memories of childhood, feeling the exhilaration of one's touch, and it blankets me with a sense of security.

Relief begins to pour, blanketing my soul with warmth. A soul that has been tattered but still exists.

An existence which is unknown.

An unknown which has given hope.

A hope of healing.

And through this healing I will fear death.

And to fear death means...today I will LIVE!

Now, as my bowed head begins to lift, I feel the tender touch of one's hand sifting through my hair, as if to massage my scalp. A warm breeze caresses my face as a heavenly light appears amidst the stormy skies just as the clouds slightly part. My eyes fastened shut no more, I am able to witness bits of beauty that surround me. Then, the touch diminishes.

Wait! Wait! Am I alone again? Have the skies taken the hope that saved me? Will my journey back be a lonely one?

A strong feeling pushes out such questions before they have time to consume me once more. I can't allow feelings of abandonment to continue to present themselves.

This feeling allows me to turn my palms downward to release that grain of sand which would only grow, pulling me away from any presence of life. This intense feeling is in the comfort of FAITH.

As I stand and look back upon the path I don't remember traveling, I see in the distance familiarity. Two faces flash back to memories of a recent past. Two faces that, at one point, I felt had deserted me. They stand as if waiting for me, making no effort to run in my direction to provide the hold I so desire.

No sooner had I questioned their lack of actions than I had the answer.

It was I who had abandoned their love. It was I who had turned my back to their extended hands as I continued away from them. It was I who didn't savor their touch!

They traveled as far as possible without taking themselves down with me.

Now I run like a toddler taking his first steps, stumbling and falling while scraping my knees and scarring my hands. From this I will not be deterred, and will have to take the steps they are unable to take. It was I who walked away from them.

Their love for me spreads through my body as I reach my destination and feel their touch. Their love for me has taken them along my journey with me until they could go no further. They are here now, but with visible wounds.

Feelings of humility overcome me, for these wounds were created by me. Through it all, my feelings of brokenness have been temporarily set aside, for their hold has shed their forgiveness throughout my soul. The wounds they endured were solely and simply their love for me.

Had I stepped into the sea, I now realize, they among others would have been left with lacerations and open wounds...never to heal again.
THERE IS ALWAYS HOPE!

THREE

The lasting impact of a suicide is devastating. Not only is it devastating to a family, it can have a major ripple effect within a school as well as a community. Questions are asked, and there is lots of speculation regarding who is to blame. What isn't seen or heard are the silent conversations within an individual's mind before and after such an act is committed.

Once the life of a loved one has been lost, there is a core group of individuals who were close to him or her in one manner or another. One may be a family member—a parent or sibling. Another could be a close uncle, aunt, or even cousin. Those closest begin asking themselves where they missed a sign. They ask themselves, "Why was I so caught up in my own shit that I didn't recognize that this person I loved and cared for wasn't willing to come to me?"

There are then those who are close in other ways, such as coaches, teachers, counselors, and the most obvious, close friends. Someone has to be blamed, right?

WRONG!

I was 17, a senior in high school, when I was first impacted by suicide. After this life-impacting loss, I felt the guilt of responsibility for the loss of a family member to such a choice. The first question I had following my family's loss was, "Could I have prevented this?" The second question was, "Was this my fault?"

As you read the story, you'll see why I asked myself these questions.

FOUR

Richard's Story

In the fall of 1989, at the beginning of my senior year of high school, I had to give a speech in English. I was in deep thought about the topic, and my wheels were turning fast.

"This is seriously one hell of a topic that Mr. Ayub wants us to give a speech on," I thought.

Is suicide a selfish act or not?

At 17, I knew everything, just as every other 17-year-old does. I was a young man who believed that nothing but success was in store for my future, even though I had no plan in terms of where my life was going.

I was captain of the football team at Williams High School in the small town of Williams, Arizona. This town was also the home of my parents and the majority of my family. The amount of time I was given to prepare for the speech is a blur, but the week before I delivered it lies embedded in my mind and heart as if it were yesterday. For reasons that I didn't know at the time, God was using a school assignment to prepare me for a topic that would become far too familiar in my life.

Viking football had been struggling for several years; we had our asses handed to us my sophomore and junior years. As seniors, we started our final year with our third head coach since my sophomore year, and because of this, expectations weren't very high. To be honest, I was hoping to have a .500 season in order to at least experience a few wins before my high school career came to an end.

The upcoming game would be a huge test for us. The number two team in the state and one of our rivals from prior years, the Bagdad Sultans, were coming to town. Times were getting exciting in our small town. The prior week, we ended the 5-year home field winning streak of Arizona's third ranked team, so this game would show the state whether or not our prior win was a fluke. Finally, Viking Football might just be for real; we were about to be tested.

During the week of preparation for our big game, my mind was silently elsewhere. Thoughts of my speech on suicide consumed my heart and mind. I took the upcoming assignment to heart, and my mind battled to answer the question of whether or not suicide is selfish. I wondered if that would end up being my concluding point because it was initially the starting point.

"Is suicide really a selfish act? Of course it is," I sternly thought to myself. "Why the hell would someone be able to justify taking his own life as an act that would never be considered selfish?" I then thought to myself, "Someone who takes his own life is creating horrific pain for others, and this is nothing short of a major sign of weakness and selfishness."

As humans, we all have instincts and feelings on which we base our opinions at any point in time. Without the willingness to truly examine the topics, let alone never have a brush with a dilemma related to one of them, we tend to stand cemented in our stance. I've come to realize that, for me, to never dive deep into a topic or issue but boldly speak up on my stance toward it anyway is ignorant.

Until you've actually walked in another's shoes, do you truly have the right to say what is and isn't right?

This question was one I learned from my parents while I was growing up. My initial opinion about the selfishness of suicide was based on minimal information I've gathered and interpreted over the course of my life. My fear of looking ignorant was important enough to cause me to dive deeper into the topic for this speech.

"Now, if I were to take my life, would others consider that selfish? Would *I* consider it selfish?"

These questions gave me the basis from which to dive in. I'd been fortunate in my life up until this point. It wasn't full of rainbows and roses, but it definitely wasn't full with tragedy, fear, and darkness either. Though my parents were divorced, I knew they were proud of me and wanted the best for me. My mom busted her ass to give my younger brother and me love and provide experiences that have carried over into my role as a father. As for my dad, he showed his love in different ways, but he wanted the best for his sons and proved to be there when he was needed.

All four of my grandparents were still present in my life, along with an endless number of uncles, aunts, and cousins. I had several other bonus moms and dads, as my parents' friends were extremely influential in my life and had plenty of opportunity to act as if I was one of their children while I was in their presence. This is one of the beauties of a smaller community, to be cared for and steered in the right direction by others. It's a huge part of why I loved growing up in Williams.

"Yes, if I were to take my own life and close the book of life too early by my own choosing, this act would definitely be labeled a selfish act," I decided.

It was time to dive deeper by looking around not only our community but the world as a whole. There are many others in this world who are not as fortunate as I was. Life in the ghetto, the hood, or the barrios was unknown to me. To not have a parent show affection or provide direction because he or she didn't give a shit about me was a reality I was unable to fathom. What about a young child who was being abused behind closed doors, physically and mentally? Or, what about people who are living on the streets, having lost everything, and are at the same time seen by others as an obstacle or nuisance to society rather than a soul needing to be saved? In exploring this topic, I essentially took away the advantages I *did* have in my life up to that point, and in doing so, I didn't like what I was realizing.

I can usually find a firm point to stand on when it comes to an argument, but the uncertainty of my thoughts and emotions caused a major internal battle. In thinking through it, I realized that I was even more blessed than I had initially realized. While this realization brought about a major change of heart, it still left uncertainty regarding my overall stance on the topic.

As a kid, I learned that we are all different by watching my dad interact with other kids while he coached Little League Baseball. His biggest asset was the way he treated each kid as an individual, and he did so by paying close attention to their personalities. He had a strong sense about their lives outside of baseball, and that influenced the way he coached each as an individual. He took the opportunity to praise every kid in the way that would most resonate. He also pushed them beyond their abilities.

As I was growing up, men who were 18 or older would stop by my house looking for my dad. They shared with me how he influenced their lives. They weren't only from Williams. They also came from the nearby towns of Ash Fork and Seligman. Each of them shared with me how my dad had impacted their lives beyond simply coaching them in the game of baseball. He also coached them in their approach to the game of life. As a kid I was proud, but it wasn't until I grew older that I fully realized the importance of the ways in which we are molded from a young age, and how many people play a role in this critical activity of influencing others as they grow up.

Each scenario in life is different, and having recognized this, my initial opinion had changed. In certain circumstances, the act of suicide was indeed considered selfish in my eyes. In many other scenarios, I might not consider the act selfish. Oh, the dichotomy of an opinion on such a powerful topic! The important question—which I couldn't fully answer—was, if my life were different and my realities were unfathomable, would I ever consider ending my own suffering?

Shit! I didn't fully know how to speak to the topic. Did my presentation have to answer one way or another, or could I just share my general thoughts? I finally chose my approach for the speech. I decided to stick with the original game plan, as this week had held a great deal of significance in several ways. For one, I wanted to nail the speech. For another, we wanted to send Bagdad home with a loss to let the state of Arizona know that Williams had a football team that was here to make a statement. That statement was that we were contenders, even though in the beginning we never fathomed the season playing out as it had.

The next question caused a wave of emotions to make their presence known to me.

"What if someone I *knew* were to commit suicide?"

How would I react? What would I do if someone in my family were to take their own life? Who would it be? Would it be my brother Lawrence? He had no reason to do so; he was in eighth grade. Why would he do that?

I then considered my parents. Would my dad take his own life? Though he battled his demons from the Vietnam War, I didn't have a strong feeling that he would ever do such a thing. "How about my mom?" I wondered. Probably not, as my brother and I weren't the worst, even though I knew I had caused her some major stress in prior years.

For some reason, my focus was most intently on my family when it came to the dilemma of suicide. "Would it be any of my uncles, aunts, cousins, or even my grandparents?" My thoughts raced. Feelings of fear and emptiness began filling my mind and heart. For some reason, this was becoming all too real. By Wednesday night, I was tossing and turning in my bed. This feeling that had consumed me was feeling more realistic than I could've ever imagined. "Why am I having this feeling, God?" I prayed aloud. "Who is going to take their life? Am I supposed to be the one to save them?" I wondered. After tears flowed on both Wednesday and Thursday night, I prayed to God, "Please take these feelings away, and help me end these emotions that feel so real!"

Friday morning arrived. There was no news of any of my family members having taken their lives. Bagdad was coming to town, and we had to take care of business. It was time to end these childish thoughts born of some fear I had created for whatever reason. Otherwise, I would let my teammates down by not performing that night, bringing back the all-too-familiar feeling of losing. I never shared these emotions and thoughts with anybody. I was quietly embarrassed, but damn, the feelings were real and hard to ignore.

I don't remember how well the speech went. It wasn't my main focus, as my mind was committed to thinking about the night's game. Besides that, it was time for this suicide shit to be done! "Time to man-up, Eddie, and get over your childish thinking," I told myself. "Here you are, a senior, a captain, and the quarterback of this team, and you've been whining these past few nights. You need to be a leader, and showing signs of weakness is not setting the right example." There was a major battle going on within me, but it was time to get caught up in the present of *what is* and *what can be*, rather than the negative possibilities behind *what if.*

When Saturday morning arrived, I woke with a feeling of grace. I rolled out of bed as if a ton of weight had been lifted off of my shoulders. "See, nothing happened." I told myself. "That speech really got to you. What the hell were you thinking, and most importantly, why the hell were you crying like a baby these past few nights?"

The day brought about great feelings of accomplishment. We defeated the number two team in state—as well as our rival—and also, nobody in my life had taken *their* life. It was a win-win ending in terms of the series of emotions I had battled the prior week. The weekend was here, and it was time to chill and soak in the accomplishments. Williams High School football was now on the map of Arizona's contenders as my uncle, childhood friends, and I looked forward to a reality we'd never fathomed—being considered one of the top teams in the state of Arizona in our respective division.

Saturday night was a night to chill out, and I decided to head to my girlfriend's house to movie-fest it with her and her family. As the coolness of fall's air was making its presence known, I decided to stop at Center Stop Mini Mart (where I worked) to grab my usual drink of choice, Dr. Pepper. After chatting it up with those inside the small town's store, I saw my uncle as I pushed opened the wood and glass doors to the outside. My mom's youngest brother, my Uncle Teddy, was more like a brother to me. He is a month younger than I am, and we were together all our whole lives up until that point. After seeing that he had been waiting for me, I walked up to his vehicle.

"What's going on man?" I asked, as I thought he was there to see what was up for the night.

"Dude, I'm sorry to hear about your cousin," he said.

Feelings of strong emotion surged through my body as I began questioning which cousin on my dad's side of the family something had happened to. "What the fuck are you talking about...which one?" I asked.

"You didn't hear? Shit! Your cousin Richard died last night, man. I'm sorry, I thought you knew!"

While I was pretty sure I knew the answer, I still had to ask. "What happened, how did he die?" My first thoughts tried to convince myself that perhaps there was a vehicle accident or even some freak accident, but I had a strong inkling of what he was going to say next.

"Sorry man. He killed himself."

I was still stunned, although I had somewhat envisioned something like this happening in the previous days. "Fuck!" I responded. "Thanks for letting me know." I jumped into my mom's black 4Runner and drove the loop around town we called the Idiot Loop.

"How the fuck could I have let this happen?" I asked myself. "Eddie, you knew this was coming, and your cousin needed you. God let you know, and you not only failed your cousin, you failed the rest of your family," I thought to myself as I drove the loop around town.

I immediately blamed myself because I was given a heads-up for some reason, and I could have, *should* have, been the one to do something about it.

But I didn't.

"How was I to know? I didn't even know where he had been living for the last year since he stayed with my mom, brother, and me the year prior." I was battling with myself. My mind was bombarded by emotions and questions. Quick waves of bitterness and sorrow set in.

"Poor Consuelo!" I thought. Richard's younger sister had now lost her older brother. My thoughts then turned to my grandmother. "This is going to kill Grandma," I thought. She'd already lost two of her eleven children, and now her oldest grandchild had taken his life.

The tears then flowed. Something told me I wouldn't have been able to save him, but I was still supposed to be preparing for this. "Why me?" I asked whoever might be listening inside the otherwise empty vehicle. To this question, there was no answer. It was something that I didn't understand, and would only come to understand in time. That ultimate understanding didn't take away the pain, but it reduced the guilt that had immediately consumed me. I dried my eyes and headed to my girlfriend's house, not telling her what I had just learned. She knew something was up, but I told her all was well and I would tell her the next day.

On Sunday morning, I opened up the Center Stop Mini-Mart at 6:00am as usual, but this time I was fully empty inside. I tried my best to ignore what had happened, but the slow morning left me alone with my thoughts, which wasn't a good thing. As the day progressed, I shared with my boss and a maternal figure what had happened. "Why don't you head home? We'll take care of the store," she offered.

"I can't. I need something to take my mind off of this," I responded. "I think I'll go to Flagstaff later, though, to watch a movie with Amy." After work, I decided to head to Flagstaff, which was 32 miles away, to watch a movie with my girlfriend after calling her and telling her what had happened.

The following week was our "bye" week for football, thank God. I have no idea how I would've handled a game at that point. I still attended practice and tried to stay focused, knowing that Richard's funeral would be in the near future. Guilt continued to creep in. The pain was incredibly present given my internal battle the week leading up to my cousin's last day. Still, nobody knew I'd even had those thoughts or emotions prior to Richard taking his own life.

I don't remember much of the funeral other than standing in the aisle of the Catholic Church in which I was once baptized and confirmed and later served as an altar boy. "I wish I could talk to you one last time, Cuz," I tried to tell him through my thoughts. Five others and myself prepared to roll his casket down the aisle. "I'm sorry, Cuz, I let you down." It was time to say goodbye to the oldest of the Aguilar cousins, the one who was named after my dad.

There are times when we feel like we are alone and nobody is paying attention. We hurt, and we believe that nobody will understand the pain we hold within. We purposely seclude ourselves from others so we can tend to our struggles through what we view as strength, when all along our weaknesses are slowly chopping us down. When we do this, we should actually be screaming out. These are the times when we need others more than ever. Going it alone is a great deal tougher than pushing through with needed help. Unfortunately, not everybody has somebody he can immediately turn to, but the need to seek guidance and support should not be shameful.

Later that evening, we gathered at my aunt's and uncle's house with good food, family, and friends. To be honest, I was hurting and becoming a bit pissed off. "I let my cousin and family down. I'm going to tie one on, and nobody is going to tell me any different!" I thought. I was ready to get hammered and numb.

Hanging out in the back room with the bar, the pool table, and a group of friends, I had already slammed two beers. It was my intention to attempt to hide that fact for a bit, as my dad was there as well.

"So, are you going to go for your third one?" I heard a voice ask.

I turned around and saw my dad approaching me.

"What the hell?" I asked myself. "How did he know I already had two beers? Oh well, I'm 17 and becoming a young man. Who the hell is he to tell me what to do?" I wondered angrily.

"Yeah, eventually I'm gonna grab another one." I told him.

"Look," he said. "I'm not going to tell you not to grab another one. Shit, I know where you're at, so you're gonna do what you want."

"Damn straight!" I thought.

"I know you're hurting and you loved your cousin, especially after getting to know each other more last summer. You can get all liquored up, but how the hell is that going to help you? As a matter of fact, how is it going to help anything? I don't think you realize what's going on in your world right now. You, your friends, and your Uncle Teddy have the opportunity to do something great for yourselves, but also for this town. You have friends and underclassman counting on you. You're the quarterback and leader of the football team, and I don't think you realize the power of what you guys have accomplished so far this year."

I was listening, as this man who I was initially ready to battle with slowly began placing cracks in the wall I had built around me, which happened to be made of glass.

"You want to honor your cousin?" he asked. "Do something in honor of him. Give him something to be proud of! You think getting fucked up is going to make him proud? Or do you think he'd rather see you excel in something that would make him proud to call you his cousin who has an opportunity to do something he didn't have and won't ever have the opportunity to do?"

"Shit," I thought.

"If you choose to sit in pity and sorrow, you're not letting me down, but you'll be letting him, your football team, and most importantly, yourself down."

"DAMN!" I thought

"The choice is yours son," my dad ended. Then he walked away.

I didn't realize until later that my dad was, in a subtle way, calling me out on my belief that I was a man. If I was man enough at the age of 17 to get all liquored up, was I man enough *not* to reach for the third, then fourth, then fifth beer, until I'd drunk myself numb? He knew me well enough not to tell me what to do, but by speaking to me as a man, he was giving me the respect I felt I deserved, whether or not I actually did. He gave me insights on the repercussions of my actions and allowed me to decide my own fate. Little did I know, I was still just a boy.

Given all that had happened in the prior weeks, I realized that God was using that time to prepare me to deal with

Richard's death. Had he not, I can assure you that my actions in response would have been different. The pain I felt that week was Richard's pain, feeling alone and afraid. Unfortunately, the relief I felt Friday night was not fully based on the outcome of the game we had played, but also the fact that the suffering he was enduring no longer existed.

After a death, God is often discredited by many. If there is a God, why would he have allowed this to happen? Why would God allow good people to hurt? Why would they never take into consideration that maybe He had tried to save our loved one many times prior? God easily becomes the scapegoat, proving he doesn't exist at all, right? Yet, somebody needs to be blamed for our hurt and anger. This fact creates contradiction in our heads and hearts, and it causes a great deal of conflict in our lives.

"Why couldn't God have saved my cousin?" I asked myself continuously. "Why couldn't I have saved my cousin?" was typically my follow-up question. I do remember a moment Richard and I had in my backyard in the middle of the night as we lay on sleeping bags on the splintered wooden deck below the low-hanging limbs of an apple tree. Thoughts of no longer existing in this world were running through his mind as tears rolled down his face, visible by the light of the moon. A year later, I realized that these thoughts probably filled his every day since that conversation, and that hurt me.

Richard had fallen into a dark and chilling place. He felt alone. When one is in that place, the world around him becomes non-existent. Loved ones escape the mind, as the world seems to spin recklessly. I can only speculate as to where he was in his mind when he made his final decision. I hadn't walked in his shoes. The life he knew was one I couldn't fathom. He grew up in Los Angeles, and I was just a small town boy. To declare whether or not his death was selfish didn't come to mind. The fact was, he'd left us, and I could and can only pray that, somehow, God had grabbed him by the nape of his neck and taken him to a place of peace.

After the conversation by the pool table with my dad, I felt as though I was standing in a valley with multiple peaks to climb. I could stay stagnant in my place of discomfort, hurt, and guilt, or I could begin climbing. I chose to leave the third and fourth beers for someone else as I leaned toward my Uncle Teddy and lifelong friend Carlos Zabala, creating a path on the football field. I wrote in black marker "4 U Perez" on a strip of athletic tape and taped it to the rear of my helmet to let everyone know who was playing with me on that field. A black strip of cloth was placed upon the left shoulder of my white jersey as an added piece of armor in memory of my cousin. Richard became my motivation when we struggled in a game. He reminded me that, despite his size (he was short compared to me), he had fight like no one else I'd known. He could've easily thrown me a "beat down" if he felt he needed to in order to keep his younger cousin in line. This dude knew how to handle himself. After all, he'd grown up fighting.

Football became the healing medicine I needed, and his moments of weakness became my strength during this time. We were not, by far, the strongest, fastest, or biggest team in our division. We were scheduled to be the opponent for multiple homecoming games, expected to give the home teams guaranteed victories. Shit, we were even ranked fifth when we met the number one team in the state in the semi-finals. There were only four teams left in the playoffs. But there was one thing the other teams never considered: we were too stupid to know better! We wouldn't go down without a fight.

We had been beaten down for a few years by others, and we were going to make them remember us, whether through a win or a loss. Defeat had become well-known in the game of football for us, and I now had a taste of defeat in life. Pain and struggle along with doubt and fear were aspects of life we needed to face.

Screw the expectations of others who choose to doubt us. If we are choosing to set low expectations of ourselves, why is that so?

We made it as far as we could--the championship game, having beaten the number one team in the state the week prior. A perfect story, right? Truth be told, we didn't win the game. But we didn't lose either. For some stupid reason, Arizona allowed a tie to be the final result of the championship game. Co-champs for the state of Arizona became our new title. Bittersweet in many ways, but truly not the most valuable aspect of the season. The season's value was defined by the ups and downs we faced. Two major injuries to two of our star players laid strong doubt to our chances, but to be honest, the fact that we were still playing pissed the rest of us off. Had we not made it to the end, or had we flat-out lost the championship game, it would've been justified and understood, but we weren't going to settle for that.

The journey held a higher value than did the destination. Our journey laid a foundation for the following seasons that we never expected to reach. We were the unexpected co-champs, and we'd surpassed everyone's beliefs and doubts. To have given up and sulked in self-pity would have been selfish of me. It may have been only football to many, but to me it brought about the realization that, following the darkest of nights can be bright days. Following pain and sorrow is an opportunity for true joy. The season, just like life, provided many obstacles and doubt, but most importantly, it provided opportunities for several of us to surpass our own expectations.

Named after my dad, Little Richard left this world at his choosing. This act didn't make him weak, he was just a young man caught up in a moment of weakness.

"Is the act of suicide selfish or not? Was I to blame and at fault for the loss of my cousin?" These questions again made their way into my mind. In my eyes, the answers can't ever be determined by me alone, as there is always a backstory of which we aren't aware. I do know this, however: the act of suicide leaves many unanswered questions, and closure is a feeling that will never be found.

I silently held onto these feelings of being the one at blame, and I realize now that I never truly shared my deepest thoughts about my cousin's passing. I have shared this story multiple times, but I have never truly faced the fact that I placed some of the blame upon myself.

So what does this mean? It means that many of you who may have lost a loved one to suicide likely know exactly what I'm speaking about. It means you are not alone, but it also means that it is more common than not to feel some sort of guilt or shame for what you did or didn't do.

If you are in the middle of your shit storm as you're reading this, let this serve as an example of what dark feelings might befall your loved ones if you follow through with escaping your dark world by your own hands. Yes, you may be free of pain if you follow through, but I can guarantee that the pain your loved ones will feel following your departure will be ten times as strong as that which you are feeling.

As my dad shared with me, "We have a choice."

Whether we are in the pit of darkness or have lost someone to the pit, we have a choice as to how we choose to move forward. Yes, I personally lost sight of this, as you read when I described the time I came came face to face with the darkness that suppressed any presence of light in my life.

I pray you find a message within this book that brings the slightest shift in perspective and allows you to continue to fight on, no matter where you are in your life at this exact point. It's possible that none of what you read in this book applies to you or your life, but that doesn't mean that there isn't an answer or insight available for you. Your willingness to dive into this book reveals a critical perspective you may have missed: YOU ARE IN SEARCH OF ENLIGHTENMENT, PEACE, AND UNDERSTANDING. This alone is a beautiful thing.

Blessings to you, and may you find peace by releasing any

guilt you hold onto for the loss you've encountered or for the darkness you feel. Remember:

> "All the darkness in the world cannot extinguish the light of a single candle."
> —St. Francis of Assisi

Just because we flicker at times, it does not mean that our light has been extinguished.

FIVE

But he himself went a day's journey into the wilderness and came and sat down under a broom tree. And he asked that he might die, saying, "It is enough: now, O LORD, take away my life, for I am no better than my fathers." And he lay down and slept under a broom tree.
—*1 Kings 19:4*

Whether or not your beliefs are based in Christianity, and whether or not you follow the Bible, you can't deny this as one of the oldest pieces of writings in existence.

The above scripture was about a man who himself wanted to die. Though he didn't express that he wanted to do so at his own hands, he prayed to God to allow him this wish. This piece of writing isn't one whereby we can reach out to its author to confirm its true meaning. Nor is it a piece of writing about which we can reach out to a generation or two after these words had been written to inquire as to whether the intended message was passed down.

The point of the passage is this: "You are not alone in your thoughts, at times wishing to no longer exist!"

1 Kings Chapters 17-18 is a story of a man named Elijah,

the "right hand man" of God in this story. He has been called upon by the most high to send a message and was given the capabilities to perform miracles of sorts. Shoot, were this to happen to most of us, our reaction would be, "You know it, I've been called upon by God. Yep, He called upon me. I am blessed for sure!"

But let us bring this story into the context of you and your life today. Let us bring this story to those loved ones we've lost to suicide. Let us bring this story to every person who walks the face of the Earth. We have each, at one point in time, been granted the power and ability to do something great. The sad truth is that we often fail to realize or recognize those gifts, especially when we are bathed in sadness, sorrow, and deep pain.

There's a man who, at one point in time, served this country and stood boldly during those moments when he felt most powerful. Unfortunately, he got to a point where he forgot the powerful mindset through which he once stood. Fortunately, this man's wall was brought down so that he could live on.

It was an emotional day as a good friend of my dad spoke at the cemetery (after initially turning down the opportunity). My dad had spoken highly of this man, but he didn't want to speak at first, nor did my dad's two other best friends, which was understandable. They all had lost a good friend, a man they use to throw down with against others on 5th street in Williams, Arizona. Some of these men were fellow soldiers who fought in the Vietnam War. Many of them had similar stories, such as divorce and invisible scars, and they had hard, leather-worn skin due to the roughness of the lives they'd lived.

The man they mourned was my dad.

There were several powerful moments that occurred that morning. One fact I realized before giving the eulogy was that many of the men I had looked up to and respected for years were hurting in a major way. They all told my brother and me to come to them with whatever we needed. They all meant it, and I know that to this day their offer still holds true. Thoughts of the man who had just passed brought tears to the eyes of many, as they knew conversations with him would no longer be had. I felt my dad's presence and shared with these men that they could call upon me as well if they ever needed anything.

On this day, I was reminded of some guidance my dad had shared with me several years prior after my Uncle Andy had passed away. My uncle, one of many I've been blessed with, was a younger brother of my mom and the one I spent the most time with growing up. I'd chosen to honor him by naming my son with a combination of his and my dad's names: Andres Richard Aguilar.

"I know you're hurting," my dad said after I called to let him know that Uncle Andy had passed. I was in my late twenties at the time. "I need you to know something, and you may not like it, but here it is," he said. I silently held the phone as I listened to him through the noise of the hospital's halls.

"Your mom has just lost her brother. Your Aunt Laura has just lost her husband. Your grandma has just lost her son. Your uncles have lost their brother. Your brothers have lost their uncle. Out of all of you, someone is going to need to step up and take care of business. You're going to have to find a way to mourn on your own and take care of all that needs to be taken care of. I know he meant the most to you because of all the time you spent with him growing up, but you can honor him by stepping up and allowing others to grieve."

There are times in our lives when we find peace outside of our own pain. Yes, we may initially tend to ignore our pain, but in helping others who are hurting just as we are, we may find some healing.

Losing my Uncle Andy was incredibly hard. And now, I had lost my dad, the man who encouraged me to help hold up everyone else when Uncle Andy had passed away. My dad was a man who found it hard to say the words "I love you," but he still showed it in his own ways. He was a man who created a great deal of tension in me as a kid, given that he was waging many internal battles due to what the Vietnam War had brought to his world. He was a man who brought different life perspectives to the children he coached and the men and women he spoke with at the counter of any bar as he sipped his nasty Coors in a can (apologies to you Coors drinkers!).

On this day, in order to honor my father, I did my best to keep my composure as I walked up to the altar. I had the honor of sharing my thoughts about the man we'd lost. I stood before those sitting silently in the pews I had once served as an altar boy. I realized this day wasn't just about me or my father. This day was about all of those who knew him.

I lost the man I had known as Dad after I'd turned only 40 years old. More importantly though, some of those in attendance had lost someone even more significant. He was the second oldest of 11 children and the oldest male. He was a big brother to many. He was the oldest uncle to the many grandchildren my grandparents had been blessed with. He was a brother to many childhood friends he'd grown up with in the small town of Williams. They knew him as a kid, when they'd together race their rides south of town in Barney Flats as high schoolers. He was a man who was there for them through their divorces, their losses, their struggles. He was a man they could talk to in the smoke-filled bar at Cordova Post 13 Legion and the world famous Sultana. The hardness these men carried was broken down through their conversations with one another. All of this I shared during my eulogy to honor the man I called Dad, the man they called Friend.

The service, which was held a few days after my dad passed away, was attended by many friends and family. We honored him at the family's plot at the cemetery just west of town in Williams with a powerful seven-gun salute. After attending the church and cemetery, I walked into the smoke-filled bar knowing my dad would never again sit down to order a drink and check on everyone. My dad's younger brother, my

Uncle Eddie, called me over to share something of importance.

"Hey, I need to tell you something," he said, with his always serious Aguilar tone. "I'm not telling you and your brother what to do, but I wanted to let you know about a promise your dad made. His friend is here, I'm not sure if you know him, but your dad promised him a cane." My dad had several canes he'd handmade, and he used them to aid him while walking since he'd taken a bullet in the hip area during the war.

"I don't know what cane, but he's going to ask you about it, and I want you to know he's not full of shit. I was there when your dad told him he'd give him one." Short and to the point as usual.

I then went to my brother and told him of dad's promise. My brother responded, "I'll run home and grab one for him."

"Bring him one worthy of what dad would give him," I said.

A bit of time went by as my brother fulfilled our dad's promise. I still hadn't met the guy my dad had conversations with while sipping Coors from a can.

"So, you're the oldest son of my friend," a man spoke to me as he walked up.

As I looked at him, I noticed that he had a gruff but warm grin as he held his new possession: my dad's cane. "I'd like to talk with you, as I've always heard so much about you from your dad."

"Definitely! Lemme grab a drink and let's sit down." I headed to a table near the window with a newly made Jack Daniels and Coke to sip on.

As he had approached me and forced a smile, I could see that his heart had been pierced once again due to the passing of a man he respected. It was a rough moment for many men who seemed to have rough exteriors but easily hid behind their quietness or, at times, portrayed a loud confidence as they disguised their struggle.

I watched and listened to him as he shared stories of

laughter and the moments of conversation that meant a great deal to him as he and my dad sipped their cold beers in the small bar of the Cordova Post 13. One thing I noticed was the way he was very careful about opening up. As he felt himself letting his guard down by sharing his stories of conversation, he would catch himself and attempt to put back on the armor he used to protect himself.

He and my dad were both Vietnam Vets who met later in life and became trusted friends through conversation. They understood each other. They knew each other's pain, and for that they were brothers bonded through beers. The man before me sat in extreme pain, and one could see that life had brought him a great number of challenges. He was hurting, as the man he once confided in had left this world.

Full of exhaustion and a heavy heart, I sipped on my Jack and Coke as I listened to the respect this man had for my dad. He pepped up as he shared stories of conversations they'd had. He thought so highly of my dad, in fact, that he once brought his friends to town to meet him.

There was a similarity I recognized between myself and this man sitting across the table from me in the smoke-filled room. As I responded to his stories with questions, he was guarded. The "guard-up" switch flicking to *on* at the drop of a hat was easily recognizable. No wonder these two men had the bond they did; this trait was part of their make-up. I've witnessed these traits before in several men, mainly veterans—most notably, my dad.

When I was growing up, my dad once asked me what I felt a true man was.

"Do you think the guy who could kick the most ass is what defines a man?" he asked as I remember churning over whether there was a right or wrong answer. "Or do you think it's the guy who gets laid the most? Is that what defines one as a man?" he asked. Then a slew of possible answers were thrown at me: "Big house, fancy cars, the most money… What do you think makes one a man in today's world?" continued to be asked as I continued to think about it. My answer to this question would allow him to begin shaping the man I would, from that point, continually work to become, so he needed to find out what kind of foundation had been set.

A man gives respect first, without demanding it in return. Respect isn't something to be earned, even though many say one "has to earn my respect." If you follow this philosophy, you respect no one until they've "earned it," and you will place people beneath you, as if they have to rise up to your expectations or whatever the hell standards you set. In my eyes, if this is his philosophy, he can keep his respect to himself!

"A man," my dad shared, "goes beyond his duties for those in need, not for self-satisfaction, but the well-being of others. He raises his kids. He stands for those who can't stand for themselves." There was a great deal more to the conversation, but my dad was molding my perspective.

This man sitting across from me had my respect well before we took a seat at the table near the window. He was obviously someone my dad had confided in and shared stories with, and if you knew my dad, he wasn't quick to share himself with others. During our conversation, I made it known that I wasn't going to pry into their talks, as I knew they were sacred to the two veterans who carried the war with them each and every day. The benefit of listening to anybody who wants to share part of themselves—no matter how small—is that you can get a sense of who they truly are.

Through the ups and downs of the conversation, as he tightly grasped the cane my brother had just gifted him, his pains were obvious. In this moment, I could see that my dad's passing might be the final nail in his own coffin if he couldn't push past them. The ink had dried, and this chapter of his life had ended with the loss of an important confidant. His book would no longer include this character who held such importance and was now a part of his past. This fact knocked the wind out of him.

After a short time, he wanted to find out about the oldest son of the man he called a friend. As he sat attentively, I shared the stories that I knew he'd want to hear. I shared the stories of influence my dad had. The stories of how my mom and dad were so forgiving of me and had always stood by my side. Several short stories were shared, from a son's perspective, about someone we both cared for. Following the conversation, he asked what I did for a living.

"Well, I do tree work and some photography, and until this past week I was half-ass working on a book about the effects of suicide," I shared with him. "The book was going to be about how suicide has impacted those left behind." At this time, I had been impacted either directly or indirectly by more than 10 suicides, the first having been my cousin.

He gave me his full attention. And as he did, I could feel an uncomfortable energy coming from him as he began squirming in his chair while grasping his cane.

As I was about to tell him that this book and topic of suicide was going to be set aside for good, he asked, "Well, how would you like a testimony for your book?"

"Fuck!" I thought, as I looked to the ceiling, knowing where this conversation was about to head. "God, you knew I wanted to get away from this," I silently whispered, sending my message toward the heavens. Then, I was reminded of the sign I was given as my dad passed, and I said to myself, "Eddie, to ask of and be given…but not give back when asked of…is bullshit. Step-up!"

As soon as the thought hit my brain and heart I knew it couldn't be ignored. "Dad, I got him," I whispered, as I knew God and my dad were watching and placing me exactly where I needed to be. I didn't like it at that exact moment, but moments of weakness are those in which many of us find our truest strengths.

"You mean you've dealt with suicide and have lost friends or family to this?" I asked, as if ignorant to the basis for his offer. I was leading him where he needed to go in order to open up and release that which was hurting him. As he stared me in the eyes, I returned his attention. The room had grown quiet despite the loud conversations going on all around us.

While sharing his pains and frustrations in life, he was still trying to guard himself from what he felt might be weakness. I emphasized that I could only try to understand, as I'd never walked his unique path. "No you haven't!" he sternly responded, as though I were going to play the caring, sympathizing friend.

After he let loose with that which was causing pain in his world, including losing his friend and having no relationship with his children, I responded in the best way I knew how. "I'm not going to sit here and tell you *not to* kill yourself," I told him in a stern voice. "From what I see, you're hurting right now, which is intensifying the rest of that which isn't right in your life. And from what you've told me, if you think nobody would give a shit if you put a bullet in your head, YOU'RE WRONG!"

His eyes opened up, as he saw a familiar energy in the younger man sitting across the table from him.

"So am I wrong?" I continued. We then sat for a short period of time in silence.

"You just told me about a group of friends you brought to town and camped with and had to introduce to my dad because they were all important to you. What about them?" I asked.

"And if not them, what about that man sitting right fucking there at the bar who told me of a promise my dad made to you so that my brother and I could fulfill that promise by giving you one of his canes?" I pointed to my dad's younger brother, Eddie, after whom I was named.

"Most important, what the fuck do you think my dad would tell you if he were sitting across from you at this moment?" I triggered some emotion in him as I delivered my points.

"Look, I'm not going to sit here and tell you not to put a

bullet in your head. But if you think nobody is going to give a shit...YOU'RE WRONG! Listen, what is going to happen is, this pain you're feeling right now after losing my dad will be *nothing* compared to the pain you will cause in the lives of those who care for you."

The advice my dad had given me when my Uncle Andy had passed took over. Someone needs to step up. Someone needs to take care of those who don't know how to handle the pain that's infesting their insides. Please understand that this approach is not for everyone, nor does it make one a hero or a stronger person than another. We see this everyday in hospitals from doctors and nurses. We see it through those who chose to serve as a police officer, paramedic, or fireman. We see it from men I've known my whole life who were once soldiers serving this country. This may even be your approach in certain instances.

After my dad's unexpected passing, I felt it was my duty to step up and do the same. Here I was, sitting across the table from a man who held an important place in my dad's life, who needed someone to remind him of the importance of *his* life. Fortunately, it was I who sat across the table from him.

I looked back across the table into his eyes and could feel his pain. It was evident, despite the wall he tried to put up to appear as though he had his shit together and was thinking clearly. "Listen, I know you're the type of man who is going to do what you want, and nobody is going to tell you different. But you and I know damn well that if you choose to close the book yourself, others will truly feel the pain you are feeling right now. So, you're going to do what it is you feel you need to do, and me telling you not to won't mean a fucking thing. You know damn well though that my dad would grab you by the back of the neck and tell you to move forward. And if he were here today and you were to pull the trigger, how the hell do you think it would make him feel?"

He bowed his head, almost in shame. I was exhausted, and beneath my breath I prayed that I had gotten through to him.

"I'm done now," I said more quietly, as I sipped my Jack and Coke.

As silence filled the air between us, we were both hurting. We had both lost a man we loved. My heart ached more for him than for myself. To see one in that kind of pain, ready to make or think about making an irreversible decision based on that pain, is truly frightening. I did care, more than he knew. He was part of my dad's life, and the cane he held onto proved their bond. The way he gripped it and admired the work my dad had put into making it showed that without a doubt.

One thing I've learned about individuals is that we are all exactly that: individuals. There is no one right answer to all the thoughts that cross our minds when we're caught up in these types of challenging emotions. I benefited from having watched my dad interact with others my whole life. I learned that some need a stern hand, while others need a bit more affection and love.

I knew that bringing a softness to this man would not work at all. He was a veteran. He'd seen and experienced what I believe must have been some really tough things. You could see he was guarded, but in a different manner than most. I prayed that the best way to get through to him was to come at him the same way he would come at another. It's never easy, but by shutting your mouth, listening, and truly paying attention, you can learn a great deal.

After several minutes, I saw his head beginning to shake left and right, and he began letting out a chuckle.

"What?" I asked.

"What is it you do for a living again?" he asked with a laugh.

At that point, we both began to laugh, knowing that the emotion caused by the loss of my dad was having an impact on us. It is times like this that the "point of impact" of losing such a man such as my dad could create a negative ripple effect. What we forget at times is that there can also be a "point of impact" that creates the kind of ripple effect that reminds us that we still have the gift of life for another day.

"You're definitely your father's son!" he said aloud with a chuckle. "Thank you, I needed this talk!" he said with gratitude.

I've learned that silence can be far more powerful than spoken words. A great deal was said following this conversation, but not a word was spoken. I may or may not have lost this man's respect, but my respect he did not lose. We shook hands and smiled as we embraced. We were grateful for the opportunity to have this conversation and share the importance that Richard Aguilar had in our lives.

The gist of this story is that there was a man who had swept his shit under the rug time and time again. I guarantee many would feel the same way when it came to some of his emotional pain, whereas others would not have allowed it to impact them in such a manner. One thing to remember is, pain is pain. The downside of this fact is that those who left us too soon felt shame or guilt in having these feelings to begin with. Even worse, and what frightens me from time to time, is the reality of what happens to individuals who aren't able to find ways to release this hurt and pain in order to move forward.

SIX

Answer me this: "Why in the hell isn't the topic of suicide being addressed in the manner it should be addressed?" The truth is that by ignoring it and sweeping it under the rug, we are doing several things, all of them unhelpful. Most notably, we're hoping that our lives are never impacted by losing someone to their own choice. Yet, when was the last time you ignored a friend or family member who might have been in need of simply knowing that they are important in the smallest of ways?

When was the last time that you learned that you lost someone to suicide and were truly shocked that this person had taken their life? Even worse, when was the last time you lost someone to suicide, knowing you never reached out to them in the beginning of their spiral down that dark, cold, slippery slope?

The truth is, we are all guilty in some form or another, including me!

From the story of Elijah in 1 Kings to my father's friend to some of the testimonies you will read in the pages ahead, a great deal of pain has been brought into this world simply because someone didn't grasp the intensity of his own or of another's pain. That same somebody definitely didn't grasp the moments of power he once held—moments that could possibly be renewed. When, in that place of darkness, one tends to forget about even those most important to him, as I did myself, forgetting the importance of my children as I place the cold steel barrel of a shotgun in my mouth.

It's time we quit hiding this subject within or behind every nook and cranny. Remember, we are all aware of it in some form or another. It's time we quit running from it and start addressing it head-on.

I am not alone in my darkness when I arrive in it and neither are you. It's time to use the power of our own voices to speak up. Sometimes, speaking up is saying, "I'm fucked up right now, and I don't know what to do!" Sometimes, speaking up is saying, "I lost someone to this tragedy of suicide, and I don't know how the hell to move on!" Sometimes, it's speaking up and saying:

"I, too was once fucked up….."

"I, too, was once lost…."

"I, too, was once frightened…."

"I, too, was in pain after losing a loved one to suicide…."

"But today, I've learned to move on in my life…..AND THIS IS HOW I DID IT!"

It's time we put our brooms away so we can quit sweeping this shit away. As a society, we need to begin by recognizing where the dirt, mess, and filth reside. We then need to arm as many people as possible with the right tools to clean up whatever is bringing filth into someone's world. Which brings me to ask, "Where are those answers are going to come from?"

From those who've survived their own darkest days, whether having almost taken their own lives or overcome the loss of a loved one to suicide, I begin. And from here, I'll pass on the baton to those of you reading and feeling this, having yet to speak up, awaiting permission.

Permission is hereby given.

It's normal to expect to feel a range of emotions following the suicide of a loved one, including anger, blame, and disbelief. When my daughter was four or five years old, she was riding her tricycle down the paved road we lived on at the time, and she crashed. She fell to the side of the tricycle and then stood up with gravel on her hands. She was scared by what had happened and realized the sting setting in on the palms of her hands.

Before she had time to allow what had just happened to process in her mind, I ran to her and rubbed her hands together to get the gravel off of them. I encouraged her to hurry so we could get back on and continue to ride. She looked at me, confused at first, but then decided to copy the actions I was encouraging her to take. Suddenly, the fear was gone, and the pain was replaced with excitement. Off she went on her cruise around the block.

One aspect of life that I quietly contemplate is that of "points of impact." Imagine, one throws a rock into the glassy waters of a pond or lake in the early morning, and a ripple effect occurs. The size of the rock determines the size and area affected by those ripples. The way the rock makes contact with the water factors in as well. The overall point is, this "point of impact," as I think about it, is a point in time wherein one's life takes a hit, positively or negatively.

These points of impact arrive in various ways, and as you think about this concept, I'm willing to bet that, as a whole, you'll likely think about what events have affected your life in different ways. When thinking about these events, if you're being fully honest with yourself—especially given the subject matter of this book—are you thinking only of the times that were negative or emotionally hard? In truth, I would be, so let's roll with that!

Divorce.

Loss of a loved one.

An argument.

Bankruptcy.
Bullying.
Being fired or laid off from a job.
Accident.
Betrayal.

The list goes on and on, right? Through all of these scenarios, the truth is that we are all individuals, and as such, we react in different ways to the same scenarios. Some of lash out in anger, feeling rage toward God and/or the world. Some of us hole up and hide our emotions internally, and the emotions become the fuel and heat that boil our internal waters. Some of us seek the blessings and lessons that might be found in such events. Some of us have no idea how to react and respond, becoming wanderers who are constantly seeking hidden answers in life, never able to fully let go of the impact that's so profoundly affected our world.

So, what do we do? How do we handle such life-changing events?

Losing a loved one, whether to natural causes or an accidental death, brings pain, hurt, frustration, and a whole slew of other emotions. The loss of someone to suicide brings about similar emotions, but there is the added reality that our emotions are intensified by the fact that someone chose to take his own life, leaving us to navigate the wake of their actions.

SEVEN

In 2013, I traveled to Las Vegas for an event called No Excuses Summit 4, a marketing seminar for business owners, network marketers, and online marketers. I had begun to experience the power of online marketing by working with a company that made personal branding websites, and I was also working with a network marketing company selling a multitude of organic products.

I attended a day party held at a gorgeous house rented by one of the companies I was working with. Many of its employees were also there to attend the summit. I was unable to attend the evening VIP parties, as I was struggling financially and barely had enough money to register for the event, travel, and eat while there. On the morning of the last day, those of us who were either dead broke or enthusiastically committed to learn from the many speakers at the event (or both) waited for the doors to open so we could gather some last nuggets of wisdom from the speakers who had excelled in their businesses.

I stood at those doors with several individuals who were also waiting to enter the massive conference room. The greatest value in these events is the the networking and connections that can be made. You shake hands and introduce yourself, announce where each of you is from, and declare what business you are in. You meet some people with whom you'll never build rapport and who you'll never see again. You also meet people with whom you form a connection. Some connections are simply business-related while others turn into lifelong friendships.

On this particular morning, I met an energetic woman from Salt Lake City, Utah named Suzette. After sharing our stories back and forth, I shared about my experiences with suicide. For whatever reason, she gravitated toward the topic, and said she'd be willing to look into it back home, as Utah was known to have a high suicide rate—especially among high schoolers. Throughout the remainder of the event, we chatted several times and traded personal information.

Within a couple of weeks of the event, I received an email from her with a link to a *Salt Lake Tribune* article referencing the topic of suicide. Though I don't remember the specifics of the article, it did acknowledge the state's high teen suicide rates. She recommended that I write a letter referencing this particular article, and told me that she would personally deliver it to the governor's office, since the governor was the one who'd brought the statistics to the public's attention. I was blown away by the immediate attention and effort she was willing to invest in a complete stranger.

I wondered why she was so willing to help me bring awareness to the topic. To my knowledge, she hadn't personally known anyone who had committed suicide, but for some reason she felt a calling to help. I wrote a response to the article, sent it to her for editing, and then put the final touches on it. Suzette had a great deal going on at the time, but she responded that she would make time within a week or two to ensure that the response was delivered.

Within two weeks, I received another message from Suzette: "Please call me as soon as you get a chance." I called her, and just after answering the phone, she said, "I know why we met. Would you be willing to come to Salt Lake to speak about suicide? I have the perfect event for you to speak at."

I was shocked. I had met this woman only a couple of weeks prior at an event in Las Vegas, and she had already secured an event at which I could speak. I was excited, but curious. I wondered why she'd said, "I know why we met."

"I'd definitely love to come speak. How soon is the event, and where would I be speaking?" I asked.

"It would be next weekend, next Saturday," she shared, which felt like pretty short notice.

"Eddie, I know why we met in Vegas. My son had just killed himself."

My heart sank. The phone went silent as her words echoed through the still air.

I don't want to speak at your son's funeral, I thought. *This isn't the kind of event I imagined.*

"I'm going to be open about this. I'm going to share the truth about this, and in doing so, maybe my son's death can help another family or save another life." she confided.

At first, I thought there was no way I could make it up there on such short notice. Money was tight—as in, very tight to non-existent—yet this woman had just lost her son and was reaching out to me. I said that I would do my best to make it happen. I then realized that this wasn't about me, and I *had* to figure out a way to make it happen. "In fact, I'll be there for sure," I confidently told her.

Thanks to the help of a non-profit and a few businesses that donated, I was able to make the trip. During the week leading up to the funeral, Suzette shared the news of her son's death with the *Salt Lake Tribune*. She shared the way her son passed and the fact that I was traveling from Flagstaff, Arizona to speak at Daniel's funeral. Unfortunately this wasn't the only thing she had going on that week.

I continued to check on her well-being, and as I imagined,

Suzette was hit by a wide range of emotions. The shock of having lost her son combined with the way in which she'd lost him was beginning to set in. Anger and frustration also showed up. The pain of him no longer answering her phone calls set in as a reality from that day forward, leaving her with no closure. The ripple effects from this point of impact began to unsettle the previously settled waters that came with having her son in her life.

Having navigated several suicides by that point, I knew what she was going through and what she would continue to feel as the days wore on. After such a loss, the tendency is for those close to the deceased to take their emotions on a detour. That's understandably more comfortable. But, if these emotions aren't faced, they will linger until, one day, they're released, causing another impactful event.

I persuaded her to allow herself to feel the anger she was feeling and tell me who this anger was directed toward. She let it out, and she didn't hold back. Her world had been shattered, and she needed to release what she was feeling.

Both anger and blame are emotions that many encounter following a suicide. The emotions are usually directed toward others. We're in search of an answer we'll never fully receive—not in this lifetime anyway. Avoiding these emotions, however, is no different from avoiding the emotions our loved one hid from until they made the decision to take their own life.

As we process what has happened, two additional emotions tends to set in: guilt and shame. They make us feel as though we should've and could've prevented the tragedy from happening. "If only" scenarios run through our heads. The guilt that runs through us is always related to our wondering whether we could've done more or whether we missed the signs of struggle in our loved one.

By the time the funeral was set to occur, Suzette had been safely talked through each of these emotions. I enticed her to be angry, but with me, not at others. This became part of the release she needed. I allowed her to feel guilt, even though it was an emotion I felt wasn't deserved. It was something she had to experience in order to find some sort of healing. Before the funeral, Suzette shared with me that, because of my help, no matter how rational or irrational the emotions seemed, she was able to safely face them.

After speaking at the funeral (which most certainly wasn't the platform I was hoping to speak at), family members shared with me the ways my words helped change how they were processing the loss of their loved one.

With both Fox News and the *Salt Lake Tribune* in attendance, I didn't want to speak to anybody until the family had said all they needed to say. I certainly wasn't there to take the spotlight in the midst of this young man's death.

As the family was being interviewed, an older gentleman approached me and thanked me for sharing my thoughts and words. "Thank you for your words," he shared as we shook hands. "They helped me a great deal."

"I'm sorry for your loss, Sir. Are you a friend of the family or a family member?" I asked.

"Neither," he responded, as I attempted to quickly put the pieces together. "My son committed suicide as well, and I read in the *Tribune* that you were coming to speak. I wanted to hear what you had to say."

I was stunned. Suzette's efforts had already proven themselves valuable. This man was in search of answers or some type of closure after his own son's death, and he was willing to show up at another young man's funeral with the hope of receiving them.

Toward the end of the conversation, I invited him to share his story with others. His response left me heartbroken. "I'm sorry, I can't do that. At my wife's request, not many know the truth behind our son's death. Many think it was an accident, and she wants to keep it that way."

Following this, he gave me a book written by U.S. Senator

Gordon H. Smith, *Remembering Garrett*, which was based on the senator's experience losing his son to suicide the day before he turned 22. I couldn't fathom what this man I'd just met and his wife had been going through, hiding the truth behind their son's death from others. I didn't judge their choice, as we all respond differently to the the "points of impact" that ripple through our lives. The emotion I believe they felt was shame. Shame is a painful feeling of humiliation or distress caused by the consciousness of wrong or foolish behavior. I'll be the first to admit that I could be completely wrong, but that was my perception based upon the information I had gathered.

We all feel shame at one point or another in our lives. Some of us feel one or the other daily, unwilling or unable to move forward from what we have done or what someone close to us has done. Shame is a cancer and a poison that will slowly eat away at us until there is no hope left—or, until one decides to let go of the emotion in order to move forward.

Researcher and author Brene Brown wrote in her best seller, *Daring Greatly*, "Shame is the intensely painful feeling or experience of believing that we are flawed and, therefore, unworthy of love and belonging." Within the book, she categorized 12 "shame categories" from her research. They include:
- Appearance and body image
- Money and work
- Motherhood/Fatherhood
- Family
- Parenting
- Mental and physical health
- Addiction
- Sex
- Aging
- Religion
- Surviving trauma
- Being stereotyped or labeled

Do any of these areas feel familiar as ones in which you might be struggling? If so, how have you handled those feelings? How have you addressed them in order to move forward despite shame's presence?

You see, there are certain events after which we should rub our hands together, allow the gravel to fall from our hands, and get back on that tricycle and ride just as my daughter did all those years ago. These events jolt us for a brief moment, but we should then learn the lesson available to us and move forward. There are other times when we must intentionally stop and be in the moment in order to gather a greater sense of what is going on or what has taken place. I have always tried to teach both of my children not to focus on the immediate impact in these moments, but to gather their breath, control their breathing, and begin analyzing the situation. At times, there is a need for an immediate response or action. At other times, we need to allow ourselves to stand still.

I don't have the right answer or approach for all situations, nor do I have the answers for each individual person going through the situation. The way I think and handle life's events likely differs from the way you think and handle life's events. Through sharing my approach, however, I hope to be able to give you a different (and helpful) perspective. The opposite also holds true. I'm a student of life just as you are, and your approach and ways of thinking may be able to help me. But nobody will learn anything if we all stay silent.

If we choose to sedate our way through issues and challenges via any one of the many escapes that present themselves to us, the suicide rate will only continue to rise. These forms of sedation consist not only of drugs, alcohol, sex, and destructive behaviors. One can easily sedate using fitness, work, or even helpful acts to ignore the emotional cancer that continues to grow inside himself while he hides from the emotions that need to be faced.

If you have no one to trust with your emotions, reach out to hotlines. Invest in counseling if you're able to. Reach out to someone you trust, and let them know that you don't need your problems to be solved, you simply need to speak and be heard. You may see your current thoughts and emotions as irrational down the road, but in the moment they are real and valid.

We all need a way to release the pressure valve, and the best way to do so is through releasing whatever is eating us up inside. Another approach I've found helpful is journaling. Writing down your deepest and darkest emotions may seem disturbing at first, but the truth is that these thoughts and emotions exist whether or not you write them down. By writing them down, you release the poison that's spreading inside of you, silently destroying you from the inside out.

For some time, friends have complimented me on my writing. When I was in my late teens, I wrote down my emotions while I was in the midst of feeling them. I'd then go back several days later, re-read what I wrote after having time to distance myself from the emotion I was feeling at the time, and recognize how absurd the feeling truly was.

The flip-side was often true as well; I'd discover just how much I was hurting. The funny thing is, being the compulsive person I am, I'd rewrite my emotions in order to tell a story, giving even more power to the exercise. That is how I began writing. It was my therapy.

EIGHT

As time went on, I discovered that I was far from alone in terms of being impacted by the suicide of a loved one. One story in particular confirmed this for me.

This story was written by the beautiful and amazing mother of one of my childhood friends, not long after her daughter's suicide. It's shaken me up multiple times over the years, and even brought me anxiety at times while working on this book.

Linda's Story

Two and a half months have passed since the death of our daughter. As I look back on the saddest, most difficult weeks that I have ever faced, I don't even know how I've been able to walk through those days. Perhaps the reason I don't know is because I didn't walk at all. Maybe it truly was as the poet wrote in the cherished words of "Footprints In The Sand."

> *"That at the lowest and saddest times in my life there were only one set of footprints in the sand." The Lord replies, "My son, my precious child, I love you and*

> *would never leave you. During your times of trial and suffering, when you see only one set of footprints, it was then when I carried you."*

When I answered the phone, I recognized our son-in-law's voice. There was something about the way he said, "Hi, Mom." That sixth sense that God gives every mom was telling me something was wrong. He began by saying that Dawn, our daughter, had been missing since yesterday. The police were notified after he came home and realized she was gone. Her purse, wallet, and cell phone were still in her room. "I'm afraid she's going to do it, Mom." I tried to reassure him, and told him we would call the church and ask everyone to pray. Then my husband Bill and I joined hands and prayed.

All night long as I prayed, my heart was filled with an icy fear. I didn't feel like I was trusting God, my faith seemed to feel like it was slipping through my fingers. "You're not acting like a woman of God tonight," I thought to myself. "No, I'm just being a mom, and I'm feeling afraid." As I lay in my bed, I thought, "Today is your 31st birthday Dawn. Please, please be alive."

The next morning came, and with it such an awareness of the presence of the Lord. In my heart the Lord whispered, "I want you to spend time with me this morning." My mind raced as I remembered it was the day I had to make all the frosting for Alyssa's Wedding Cake. Again, I felt the nudging of the Holy Spirit to go out and spend time with God on the porch swing. This was always my favorite meeting place with God, and the hummingbirds always seemed to be especially busy drinking in the nectar from the feeders that hung just overhead from the ceiling. Sometimes I wondered if God brought the hummingbirds right when I was praying because I got such a kick out of watching them.

As I sat, feeling the warm sun on my back, I was so grateful that the fear that so gripped my heart the night before was gone.

Then I heard the words that seemed to fill my whole being, "Trust in the Lord with all your heart and lean not to your own understanding." I remembered the next verse that follows, Verse 5: "In all your ways acknowledge Him and He shall direct thy path." Yet strangely, I felt like the Lord had just said Verse 5 again, "Trust in the Lord with all your heart and lean not to your own understanding." (Proverbs 3:5) Then the Lord told me to "Meditate on this day and night. Today, I will place my peace upon you."

Three days later, on August 23rd, we still had not heard any news about Dawn. Then my cell phone began ringing. When I picked it up, I heard a woman's voice. It was Dawn's friend. She was crying. As though my mind was shutting out any possibility of a conscious thought, I heard vaguely, as though her words were echoing down a long tunnel, "She's dead! Dawn's dead!" She was still talking, but I couldn't absorb anything she was saying. I felt frozen in time.

After my husband later confirmed with the police, Bill turned toward me and began to cry. He took me in his arms and said, "She's gone, honey." I don't know how long we cried. I just remember that I have never felt so much grief. The pain and emptiness and finality overwhelmed me. "Why Lord, why?" And then I remembered, just three days before, the Lord's words to me: "Trust in the Lord with all your heart and lean not to your own understanding."

The Lord was indeed preparing my heart. There are some things that we will never be able to understand, no matter how hard we try. There are some things that only our Heavenly Father understands. Those are the times when we just have to trust that God sees more of the whole picture than we do. It's like looking at the backside of a piece of embroidery. It doesn't look like anything but a lot of jumbled-up threads. One day, the Lord will let us see the "other side." In God's hands, the intricate, delicate stitches all come together to form a beautiful picture. Until then, we just have to trust Him.

Yet one thing I understood with all my heart was that, in spite of the circumstances, God was in control, not the enemy. Because our daughter had taken her own life, I imagined that the enemy might think that he had won. Somehow, something rose up inside me that wanted to put the enemy in his place and establish God's sovereignty. I wanted to demonstrate to the enemy, "You are defeated! Jesus, I don't understand, but I trust you." I raised my hands to my Heavenly Father and said, with tears still running down my face, "Lord, I worship you, and I praise you. You are bigger than my grief, and I know you'll help us through this."

Our daughter Dawn's death was the lowest time I have ever faced in my life. Yet it was during that time that I know that I have felt my Heavenly Father pick me up and carry me between His shoulders.

"The beloved of the Lord dwells in safety by Him, who shelter him all the day long and he shall dwell between His shoulders."
—*Deuteronomy 33:12*

Closure is unlikely until one trusts despite not understanding, as the answers sought have left with the one who has chosen to take his own life.

NINE

CLOSURE
A letting go of what once was.
A complete acceptance of what has happened.
An honoring of the transition away from what's finished to something
new.

FINALITY
The fact or impression of being an irreversible ending.

This is by far the part of the book that's toughest for me to write. The reason is that it's not about only one story. There is no *one* story that can perfectly address finality and closure.

Above I've defined two important words, the first being "closure." No matter which official definition you prefer, the word "closure" is just as powerful as the word "suicide" when one tries to tie it to the aftermath of a suicide.

Through the multiple aftermaths I've personally experienced, I've found that the word "closure" has been applied only in the sense that I've been able to let go of the questions to which I've sought answers. They were questions that could only be answered by one person, and that person is not—nor will they ever again be—around to provide clarity as to why they chose to leave this world.

The second word is "finality," representing an irreversible ending, whether perceived or factual. Unfortunately, we can't go back in time and change events, and we can't find answers that satisfy the loss that's impacted us.

This next testimony is from Jerry, who shares his thoughts on the loss of his younger brother, Mike.

Jerry's Story

JUNE 1991

I am 23 years old, starting a new career in a new city. After being away from my family for the last four years, I moved back to Arizona to be closer to them all. At a time when the the excitement of new challenges ahead are energizing, with one phone call it all changed—for the rest of my life.

I had been out celebrating a friend's birthday the night before, and it was around noon when the phone rang. My girlfriend at the time answered it, and the look on her face told me that something wasn't right. It was my aunt calling. She told my girlfriend not to let me out of her sight, and that she needed to speak to me. In a very calm, melancholy voice, she informed me that my little brother, Michael, was dead. I dropped to my knees in extreme confusion. The first thing I wondered was, "Was it a car wreck?" No, he killed himself.

The moment seemed to last an eternity, and it's still incredibly vivid in my memory. The hardest part was seeing my family afterward, especially my mom. There was nothing but devastation and tears from family and friends.

Fast-forward 23 years, and it still sometimes seems like a

dream. How could my little brother who had so much going for him decide to take his own life? I quit asking myself that question many years ago; the search for the answer only led to more despair because there is no answer. My twenties were spent hiding from it, masking it with a fake smile as though everything was okay. I didn't want to talk about it to my family; I felt it would only refresh the wound and cause pain. I felt like an outsider everywhere—if only people knew my dark secret. The shame I felt when I told new friends and acquaintances who didn't know my story combined with feeling discomfort from those who knew my story when in my presence. They didn't know how to address or handle the topic. It wasn't their fault; how do you address something like that? There was a lot of talk about the weather, but when somebody did confide their sadness, it was beyond touching.

I joined a group of amazing people who had been through the suicide (it's still hard for me to say that word) of a family member/friend. With them, I felt like less of an alien. Other people had felt the same extreme pain and shared it beautifully with me. Hearing about their son, brother, friend, sister, daughter or husband gave me courage to tell them my story in return with discomfort, but liberation. I am so thankful to have met them at that time in my life; I really needed their support. I was not alone. A sobering reality started to set in that if my brother had not ended his life, I may have ended my own, not knowing the devastation that such an act would bring to so many.

When I was approached to write about my experience for this book, I wasn't sure if I was ready to discuss it out loud for all to read. I still mask it often, not necessarily out of shame, but out of not wanting others to be uncomfortable. It is such a taboo subject, yet common for so many. A few years after my brother died, a musician I greatly admired killed himself. Just recently, an athlete I looked up to did the same. These are the moments when you realize that anybody is capable of this act.

Anyone is capable of having moment in which he's so stuck in his head that he can't see tomorrow and all the good that could come with it. A moment where it seems that the world would be a better place without him in it. A moment when you don't consider the countless lives your actions would impact for the rest of *their* lives. The number of lives one person can touch is truly astounding.

We've all had moments when life got too tough to comprehend, when problems seemed too big to get past. Moments when something so small to another person seemed so insurmountable to yourself. Some use drugs, alcohol, overworking, paralysis on the couch, or religion to get through these moments. I tried all of those, to no avail! I write this due to the fact that my brother could not get past that moment. If he could have seen the sadness in our mother's eyes for years to come, he certainly would never had done what he did. If he had seen the niece and nephews he has missed out on, he certainly would be here today. He was a good young man, full of love and care for his family and friends. Before I went out to meet him for what would be the last time, I told my girlfriend, "I am going to meet my brother tonight. What if something happened and I never saw him again?" That really came out of my mouth before I saw him for the last time.

My brother and I had just begun to become friends on a new level, as adult siblings. A new kind of bond was forming that I did not see at the time. We were best friends all our lives. He helped me move to Florida, and we both had dreams of moving to L.A. and working in the music industry—he as a musician, I on the other side due to my lack of musical talent. He was a good guitar player.

"Spuck" was a nickname he gave me due to my pointed ear, a reference to Spock from Star Trek. I quickly reversed the nickname onto him, and thankfully it stayed with him and not me! Our childhood was pretty "normal," whatever that means. An absent father, an amazing mother—we didn't know anything different. We did what boys do: played sports, enjoyed bb guns, etc. We had lots of friends, who are still friends to this day. Life was pretty good. He had lost a friend to suicide in his late teens, and he was a pallbearer at the funeral. I know it really upset him, wondering how that could happen. But a few years later, he decided to end his own life? A few years after that, a good friend of ours did the same. He'd been a pallbearer at Mike's funeral.

They were all good young men who could not see past the distraction of the moment. Who could not see the lives that they would impact forever. They created a permanent solution to a temporary problem.

Survivors are exactly that. We have the ability to absorb pain so great that it never goes away, but we learn to live with it and be happy again. We live with a big, gaping hole in our heart that can never be filled. We have been, for lack of a better term, ripped off. Robbed of the good times the future was ready to bring. We were robbed of the children, relationships, and aspirations that were destroyed. I never got angry at him, I just felt ripped off. My kids were ripped off by not knowing the person who would have been an amazing uncle. His friends were ripped off. And, most of all, his mother was ripped off. Who can fathom their child dying before they do, at the age of 21 and by their own choice? As a parent, I can only imagine that pain, and I don't like to think about it. I do know that he is remembered, but it saddens me that he is remembered for his violent death as well.

23 years later, I sit here and type this, and the fact that this tragedy happened to my family is still not real. Over those 23 years, I have been impacted by many others who were close to me or influential in my life who decided to take their own lives. I estimate that, if truth were told, most families have dealt with this either directly or indirectly. Strangely, I can say that I am a better person because of this, as bizarre as that may sound. Deep sadness can create a higher awareness—awareness of the

impact that one person can have on countless others around him.

The awareness that a temporary problem is only temporary and that a selfish act does not make it "go away" is not an awareness that those who commit this act have. No matter how tough the moment is, tomorrow will be better. How can it get worse, right? Only if we make it worse in our head. Either way, it is a choice. A choice to live and tough out what life throws at us, no matter how insurmountable it may seem in our head.

THE FIRST TIME I READ JERRY'S TESTIMONY, IT WAS A TOUGH read. Even though he and I sat and carried on this conversation several times, it's different when you sit down and are faced with only your thoughts. To then convey your story and emotions is not easy.

Jerry and I tried to answer questions that we both knew only his brother could answer. We can speculate all we want, but haven't you ever manipulated the truth in order to tell a different story when you're in the middle of trying to figure it out, to figure life out?

There comes a point when we need to address the truths and realities. Reality is a complete acceptance of what has happened, but it's not an understanding. The truth is, we are now faced with an irreversible ending. This leads us to live life with a scar that tends to reopen from time to time as we are caught in the lows of life, and in the highs as well. It is hard for us to simply let go, and for some it's worse to try to forget. In an attempt to forget, one sedates himself from any and all pain, not realizing that although they are sedating themselves from the pain and struggle, they are also sedating themselves from the true happinesses of life. One is not able to fully sedate and hide from one aspect of life yet simultaneously be fully able to receive the positive aspects of life.

TEN

Here is another testimony I received from Jeff, who is a close family friend.

As I answered, the voice on the other line told me my brother had been shot and to get over to my aunt's house. It was all a blur; I couldn't tell you if it was my mother or father who called me that night. I raced over to my aunt's, which was about a five-minute drive away, and pulled up to see my mom and dad standing outside waiting for me. They told he had been shot, and they were heading up to Flagstaff. My dad gave me money to fill up the gas tank, so I headed to the gas station. At this point, I assumed that my brother was still alive. There weren't a lot of details available at that moment. I remember being shocked but thinking that he was in the hospital because he stupidly shot himself in the leg or something.

I returned to my aunt's and saw my dad with his hands over his head. I just got this sinking feeling in my heart. I knew something was wrong. I got out the car and saw my dad crying.

"He's dead, mijo, Sam's dead." Those words will forever live in my memory.

"Not my brother, God no. Please not my brother!" I wheeled around and slammed my fist through my aunt's storage door and collapsed to the ground in tears. My family huddled around me, but I pushed them away and walked out into the alley, crying and screaming. I collapsed in the alley, and my father came to hold me. After some time, my parents got into the car and drove to Flagstaff. It was 1:00am or so. I stayed behind with my aunt and cousin until the morning. My roommate came to get me and drove me to Flagstaff, escorted by his sister. I couldn't have imagined driving at that point. Exhaustion was setting in.

I arrived home where my parents were, and all the sadness came flowing out again. I remember falling to the floor in the bathroom, crying hysterically until my mother came in. We were all a wreck by this time. It was during this time that I got the full story of what had happened. My brother had killed himself. He'd gotten drunk at a wedding and was pissed when the bartender wouldn't serve him anymore. He went to the truck, grabbed a gun, and pointed it at the groom. They finally calmed him down and took him home, where he continued to drink more. My sister-in-law and niece were down the street. I can't remember why. The cops came for Sam, and he barricaded himself in his room. He stripped down, laid on the bed, and shot himself through the roof of his mouth with his .38. The cops came in to find him dead on the bed. I can't fully confirm this, but it's what I recall as the news started to come out.

Years prior to Sam's death, he once told me how he would kill himself. He told me that he would shoot himself in the head through the roof of his mouth. I didn't think twice about it at the time because it was hypothetical. Like saying, "Man, if that happened, I'd slit my own wrists." That was what I assumed that comment meant. Off-the-cuff comments like that don't have the same meaning to me anymore. It's only after his suicide that I realized he figured out how he would do it because he had actually thought about it. I ask myself all the time, was that his cry for help and I missed it? Could I have done anything differently? The fact is, no, I couldn't have done anything differently.

After his death, my focus was strictly on my parents and my niece and sister-in-law. They were who I needed to get through this. I would have my time to mourn sometime in the future, but right then I needed to take care of my family. I needed to be their rock. I took care of everything I could, from making the arrangements to working out the cremation with a friend I used to work with. My parents needed to mourn, and I needed to take care of them. I was watching my parents fall apart in front of my eyes, and no matter what I did, I couldn't take away their pain. My sister-in-law, dad, and I went to the funeral home for the viewing of my brother before his cremation. My sister-in-law went in first, followed by my father. I drove them there, but didn't want to go in to see him. I remember my father punching a brick wall and breaking his hand.

After they came out, I stepped into a room I thought was empty to talk to my friend, who was the funeral director. Lying there on a table, covered in a white sheet, was my brother, eyes closed and lifeless. I accidentally went that far, so I figured I'd go the rest of the way and say goodbye to my brother. I looked down on him and studied his face as best I could. Tears welled in my eyes as I touched his head. I could still see some dried blood in his hairline. He was pale, and his eyelids looked bruised. I told him that I loved him, and I kissed him on the forehead and walked away. I was the last person to see my brother's face. That image is seared into my brain, and is as clear and vivid as though it were yesterday.

As the week went on, we had his funeral and people came out in droves to pay their respects. I remember looking out at the crowd and thinking to myself, "Damn it, Sam, if you could see how many people were here, you would understand just how much you were loved." I take solace in the fact that my family and I were supported by so many, and that my brother had many friends who loved and cared for him. For that, I am truly thankful to all the people who turned out.

I stayed in Flagstaff for a couple of weeks to help my family through as much as I could. I even thought about moving back home for them, but my parents told me that to do that was unacceptable; the opportunities to better myself were in Tempe and Phoenix. There was nothing good for me in Flagstaff. The day I left was my birthday, which happened to be Father's Day as well. It was a horrible day. I was turning 23, and I had nothing to celebrate.

I recall sitting at Red Lobster and looking across the table at my parents. They were drained and tired. They did their best to give me a birthday celebration, but it was no use. I knew then that they were broken, and they were never going to be truly happy again. Losing parents or friends or other family members is tragic in and of itself. To lose a child would be the end of the world. I now have a family, and it sickens me to even think about it. This, I think, was the moment when I started to get angry—angry for the selfishness of the act of taking his own life, and angry for the disregard for what he was leaving behind. There was anger for all the pieces that needed to be put back together, and for all the lives that would never be made whole. Then, there was disgust at the fact that my niece would grow up not knowing who her father was. It was within a matter of hours that I came to all these realizations. It was only a short time before my sadness changed into frustration and anger. I couldn't believe that Sam, through all his faults, could be this selfish. Yes, he was probably going to get arrested for assault. He would probably have gone to jail for a bit, but he would have come out afterward with a family who loved him and a beautiful daughter to watch grow. This was well before I settled down and had kids of my own. Still, to this day, it angers me that my children will never know the person I shared my life with growing up. Good experiences or bad, the fact remains that it's what shaped me and contributed to who I became.

As a result of seeing my parents suffer so much, I lost my faith in God. I had always been a little skeptical because I am more of person of science, and God and science don't usually go hand in hand. The little faith I did have disappeared overnight. My parents are religious people, so my thinking was, *How could a God who my parents worship so much cause them so much pain?* If God is the master of everything and controls everything we do, how could that be a God I would even remotely want to worship? I see them so sad, even on the best of days, and it's agonizing. So I quit God.

I had this conversation with my parents when it came to baptizing my kids. I baptized my son out of respect for my family and their beliefs. The fact is, I never wanted to do it, and I feel guilty that I did because the only positive I see in it was the cash and bonds my son got for his baptism. That's not fair to my son, nor is it fair to the people who actually *do* believe in God and gave money to my son. So, after that, I decided that I wasn't going to do it anymore. I have a beautiful wife and three amazing children who are my heart. People have told me that I'm blessed, and God has given me these gifts. I say to them, "Sorry, I have beautiful kids because my genes and my wife's genes came together and produced children of those genes." Like I said, I'm a person of science, but also, if God did happen to give me these gifts, where was He when my parents needed him the most? He abandoned them and left them on their own to suffer. That's not a God I want to worship. Out of respect for those who do believe, I try and keep my mouth shut, but there are times where I hear, "It's a blessing," and "Thank the Lord." But where was he on the terrible night? A friend of mine said, "He must have been in Africa giving AIDS to babies" because he was nowhere to be found for my parents or the rest of my family.

Out of everything that happened on that horrible day 13

years ago, most of it was bad. I lost my brother, my parents lost their son, my sister-in-law lost a husband, my niece lost her father, and one thing that still tears at me is that my father lost his best friend. They were so close and spent so much time together that, to my father, it was doubly devastating. He's never been the same. None of us have. I do take some comfort in knowing that my niece was too young to remember any of it. She'll know that her dad is gone, but the trauma of the tragedy will elude her. And for that, I am thankful.

I say all of this knowing that not everything that came out of it was bad. The tragedy that unfolded made me a stronger person. Having to cope with this type of loss awakened me to what makes life important. I would rather have learned that in *any* way other than this, however you play the hand you're dealt. Furthermore, the death of my brother brought me to a conversation with someone who had recently lost her father. I was introduced to her in a way that would let her know that she was going to be okay and could talk to someone who had been through a great loss. That person would later become my wife. So, it took two people to die for us to be together. It's a nice story and all, but I'm sure I would have met her some other way since her roommate and mine were friends from work.

As I close out these thoughts on the suicide of my brother, I try not to think about all the meanness and attitude he gave me and my family over the years. I instead think of the good times. He was a good father and turned out to be a good guy. He was my dad's best friend and sidekick. I don't try to cover up all the other parts with rose-colored glasses because that would be lying to myself. I am still angry about the whole ordeal, but now I focus on the simple fact that I miss my brother. I miss him dearly. I'm sad that he's missed out on the wonderful life that was waiting for him. There were and always would be ups and downs. There would be good times and bad, but the good greatly outweighed the bad. I'm sad that it caused my sister-in-law to move and take my niece with her. My parents lost their son along with their granddaughter to another state. The one piece they have left of him is very rarely seen.

I'm sad that he never got to meet my wife or my children, and they never got to meet him. It would have been great to still have my older brother around to share the best parts of life with. Unfortunately, I have the burden of knowing he's not around because he chose to take his own life. I still have trouble explaining that to people if they ask if I have any siblings, or having to explain to my children where my brother is and why he's dead. It's a lasting agony for all of those he chose to leave behind.

TAKE A MINUTE TO GATHER YOURSELF, AS YOU'VE PROBABLY BEEN hit by a range of emotions. I was—and still am—each time I read this testimony.

Through the testimonies, you can see the range of emotions through which suicide impacts the lives of others. It impacts those close to us as well as those we never expect to impact. The sad truth is, if we choose to take that final step, we'll never know the devastation of the "point of impact" we leave upon others.

If you're depressed and battling that which causes such thoughts to occur, *please know you're not alone*. There are others out there--many of them--who have been where you are and have turned their lives around. It's not easy, but it is absolutely possible. Though you may not feel life is worth fighting for, the truth is that it is. It may take some time for you to find out why you are to fight, but I have found that, in time, you will be provided with the answer.

It may be to save the life of another through sharing that you overcame your trials and tribulations. It may be to father or mother a young child. The answer may simply be that you will find that you are of importance to this world in some specific way. Don't allow an irreversible ending to haunt and redirect the lives of others toward one of misery, pain, and sorrow. You, my friend, have the power you feel like you've lost. You simply have to recognize it, acknowledge it, and tap into it to fight for tomorrow!

How do I so confidently know this? Remember, I felt my finger applying pressure to the trigger of a Remington 870 Wingmaster 12-gauge as my mouth was wrapped around the cold steel barrel. Yet, by the grace of God, I'm here to write this book! If I made it through the darkness, you can too.

ELEVEN

It's important to move forward with your life. You will not be resented by those left behind or by those who left.

The big question and dilemma that those left behind face is, "How do I move forward?"

Whether it's a child, parent, or friend we lose to a suicide, the pain that settles into our hearts is excruciating. The guilt, the fear, the shame that funnels through our hearts and minds keeps us in a continuous cycle of chaotic thoughts and feelings. From trying to find some type of closure to seeking the peace necessary to move forward, there are no simple steps to follow.

The main reason this idea for this book came about was the suicide of my good friend Robert, which in turn led me to almost take my own life. I watched what his mom was going through and her life altered in an unforeseen direction, and that perspective had a profound effect on me.

In April 2014, I received yet another life-impacting call. A familiar voice said, "Eddie, Mom is in the hospital." The words rang through my ears as the voice took me back to the day when

I received the call that my good friend Robert had to be pulled off of life support. Now, once again, a voice echoed through the phone; and once again, it was George, my brother's dad.

Caught off guard by the unexpected phone call, I sat at the desk in one of the bedrooms of my two-bedroom apartment as my kids made something for dinner. I was clear on who was in the hospital, but I asked for clarification with the hope that he might change his answer.

"Who?" I asked. While I never called her Mom directly, I considered her a mother figure in my life.

"Suzanne." Her name echoed as he said it. "Eddie, she had a brain aneurysm and is in the hospital. It's not looking good," George responded. His voice, combined with the news, took me back to the day when I sat at my kiosk in the mall on the outskirts of Chicago. My heart stopped as I grew flustered by the news.

After asking him several questions, I said, "Well, I have my kids, so I'll stop by first thing in the morning, George."

On the other end of the line, I heard hesitation in his voice. "Oh…..Okay."

"I'm sorry, George. I'll see you in the morning," I said and hung up the phone.

As I walked out of the bedroom and into the kitchen, I grew more flustered as my emotions and thoughts swirled. "This can't be," I thought to myself. "Poor Kelsey Morgan! First her dad, and now her Nana." I then thought about George. He'd finally gotten his wife back after Robert's death. Why did he now have to go through this? As soon as I had this thought, another one immediately came to me: "Eddie, you dumbass, why the hell did you tell him you'd be there in the morning? You're going to leave him there alone? Get up there now!"

After telling my kids that I needed to run up to the hospital because something had happened—though not to someone they knew--I called George to let him know I was headed his way. I realized that I was initially giving less intensity to the situation with the hope that, in doing so, all would be alright. "Eddie, she may not make it to tomorrow, so get your ass up there," I told myself.

On the drive, I found myself crying as I topped out on the road on Cedar Hill, the hospital in sight below the empty street. I was crying because of the pain she'd endured, beating herself up after Robert's death. And recently, very recently, she'd let it go so she could happily live the rest of her life with her husband and "oh so dear" granddaughter who had become her world, as she was a piece of Robert.

As I reflected upon the previous years, many conversations filled my mind. "Eddie, it's my fault! I should've seen he was hurting" was the constant guilt this beautiful woman lived with. "It was my responsibility as his mother to protect him and to recognize his pain" was her truth.

Each time I'd faithfully head to their house year after year to do their annual holiday photo shoot in either October or November, I knew it was going to be an emotional day. The photo shoot I did with George, Suzanne, and Kelsey Morgan took place in the fall of 2012. I remember it clearly. Kelsey Morgan had spent another year growing toward the beautiful young lady she was becoming. As for George, I could see that the impact of Suzanne's guilt had taken a toll on him. "Man," I often thought to myself, "This is what true love looks like: 'Til death do us part.'"

The photoshoots were a reminder of Robert, as they were centered around the daughter he left behind. After each one, we'd gather in the kitchen and Kelsey would wander to her room. Intense conversations would begin over a glass of whiskey or some other sort of drink as smoke from their cigarettes filled the air.

Each and every time, I'd begin peeling back the emotional layers to determine whether there were any improvements in Suzanne's perspective. This woman, who was once so strong, had become a shell of the woman my brother introduced me to many years prior. I'll tell you that, when one commits to a belief and convinces themselves of their truths, no matter how false they may be it's tough to crack their exterior. Many times over, I felt the conversation heading in the direction it needed to, but she'd catch herself and redirect back to the place that had become all too familiar.

"Have you ever been pissed with him?" I asked her one night, to which she shot me a "What the hell are you talking about" look. "What? Why would I be mad at him? He needed me, and I failed him Eddie" she responded.

"No. You need to speak out loud to him. You need to be pissed off at him for doing this to you!" I shared, as her eyes grew wide. My words made her uncomfortable, but she was living an uncomfortable life as it was.

"No Eddie, I could never be mad at him," she responded.

"Suzanne, you need to go through that emotion. He left you. He left George. He left that beautiful little girl downstairs! You need to have a moment of being pissed with him." She did not like what I was suggesting.

"And then, you need to forgive him for the hurt he's caused you. I know that, deep down, there's a part of you that would like to be pissed with him, but you feel that doing so wouldn't be motherly of you. I know that you loved him more than the world, just as you love George. But don't tell me you never get pissed off at George."

To this, she responded with a slight chuckle.

"Eddie, I wish I could truly move on. Sometimes I go days without getting out of bed. When I know Kelsey Morgan is coming over, I have to work at preparing myself for her, and sometimes I can't have her over because I don't want to get up." I listened as my heart ached for her. My heart also hurt for George, as the woman he was committed to struggled daily.

"You know, Eddie, one day at the old house, I was outside early in the morning talking to myself, kind of praying," she began sharing. "If only I could move on and be given a sign that it's okay to let this go. That's all I want."

As I listened, I could see that she was reliving the moment she was about to describe to me. It was as though I was with her in the memory as I remembered their prior home.

"I was sitting outside with my coffee on a cool morning when this bird flew onto a branch of the tree after I spoke these thoughts. As I watched this bird, I realized it was looking at me, or that's how it felt. It was a beautiful little bird, but this one was different. I felt something, but wasn't sure what it was. It watched my every movement, so I decided to walk around the corner of the house, and as I did, this bird followed me. When I stopped, it rested on the branch of another tree and watched me. Eddie, I think it might have been Robert visiting me," she shared. I could see her seeing that moment in her mind's eye once again.

"Did you ever stop to wonder whether *that* was your sign, Suzanne? If you never choose to recognize a sign as a sign, you'll never give in to those that present themselves."

"I'm not sure, Eddie" she responded. "It's just hard to let go."

"I get it, Suzanne. I truly do. Robert was with me when I was about to kill myself. He saved my life, Suzanne, and I know for a fact that I was ready to kill myself, but had Robert not already taken his own life, he wouldn't have been able to save me," I shared as tears began rolling down her face.

"I know you want your son back, but it's not going to happen. You have a beautiful granddaughter who needs her grandmother to be whole. And the man who stands right here, never leaving your side--and I know for fact that many men would've up and left by now--he needs his wife to be whole again. It's not that you can't have hurt for Robert anymore, but you need to find happiness in life again."

These conversations always took a turn toward tears, but I

think she finally was reaching the point of accepting what I was telling her.

"We both know that if Kelsey Morgan didn't exist, you'd have followed your son's path due to the pain you've endured and in order to be with Robert once again, right?"

"You know I would, but I couldn't do that to her," she responded.

"Well, what about your husband? Do you think he wants to hear that he's not worthy of you sticking around? Even though he's stood by your side all these years? Let me ask you a question, Suzanne."

"Okay," she responded. I could see that she was fighting to keep up her strength while taking on the challenge of my upcoming question.

"When you're getting ready to see your granddaughter, you paint on this happy persona for her. The persona of someone who is strong and has it all under control, right?" I asked her.

"You know I do, Eddie. I don't want her to know I'm living in pain. It would kill her," she responded.

"How is that any different from what Robert did to you. Didn't he paint on this happy face and attitude because he knew how much you loved him, and that it would kill you to know he was in such pain?" I asked.

"Yes, but I'm his mother, and I should've recognized it," she replied. I knew we were coming upon a critical moment.

"No, Suzanne! Robert was a grown-ass man, hiding his pain from not only you but the world as well. Shit, he had your stubborn-ass blood running through his body. Do you mean to tell me that he didn't do to you what you're doing to your granddaughter? You mean to tell me he didn't have the capability to do what you did today by painting on a fake smile?"

The house grew quiet. I believe that, in that moment, she finally realized that her son was trying to hide his pain from her in order to protect her, just as she had done for her granddaughter since his death.

"Suzanne, he loved you so much. He loved George, and he definitely loved his beautiful baby girl. He didn't want you to hurt, but the fact is, he didn't realize how much *he* was hurting. It just became too unbearable for him to carry. Not only being a man, but being the man he was, he was unable to reach out for help. That's not your fault, by any means. He thought he was protecting you."

The tears rolled down her face as I held mine back. I looked up to the ceiling in hopes Robert could let her know it was okay to live her life. "C'mon brother, help me out," I whispered.

"Suzanne, because you've lived with this for so long and carried the weight of it all, I think I know what scares you," I continued, as she glanced my way. "The question you have is, if you let this go, are you dishonoring your son by living a life filled with happiness? On top of that, the next question is 'Who is Suzanne from this point forward?' You can redefine your life and not be the mother of a son who committed suicide, living in darkness. You can be the mother of a wonderful son who contributed to the lives of others and even saved *my* life. You can be the grandmother who's full of life for the beautiful little girl downstairs. You can also be the wife of this great man who has stuck it out with you this whole time, knowing damn well he held true to his word of 'til death do us part!"

I felt her guard come down as I reminded her of the truth she already knew. "We both know that if Robert could have one last talk with you, he'd apologize for hurting you so much. Tell me if I'm wrong, but we both know he'd want you to be happy. To live life and show his daughter some of the things you taught him. He'd want you to show her your world and love the man who took him in as his own son. Suzanne, he would ask you to quit taking ownership of something you had no control over."

She had no response. She knew that the bottom line was that

her son had a huge heart and was a strong man who happened to fall during a time of major weakness.

The following year, we had what would be our last photoshoot. Kelsey Morgan had grown another year older, and I could see her dad's smart-ass attitude and fight as well as her mother's beautiful features beginning to take shape. I honestly don't remember the post-shoot conversation this time, but it was less intense than it had been in prior years. If I remember correctly, I had another obligation that afternoon, which caused me to leave sooner than I preferred. I figured we'd dive deeper into conversation when I returned with the photos.

As I sat at my desktop a few days later, editing the pictures I had taken, I began to tear up in response to what I saw in the pictures, which I'd missed during the photoshoot.

"She finally let go!" I spoke out loud. "She finally let go!"

I rushed through the editing of the pictures, as I couldn't wait to get back over there. I think this might've been the quickest editing turnaround time on record. I put my complete focus on getting these shots edited. I set up a time to head over to give them the disk of pictures, then hauled ass over when that time came. I was so excited, I couldn't wait to see George and Suzanne.

As I walked in, we took our usual approach, walking to the kitchen and sitting down at the counter as George popped the disk into their DVD player of their small TV. I sat back with joy as the slideshow played before us. She was thrilled with the pictures, as usual, but this time it seemed so real. I spoke up after the slideshow had fully run through, returning to a picture that, to this day, fills my heart with joy. "You let go, didn't you? You've finally moved past it, haven't you?"

She returned my question with a smile. "Yes, I did Eddie. Thanks to you."

"Suzanne, I didn't recognize this during the photoshoot, but I literally began crying when I started editing these pictures. I'm so happy for you!" I shared, as George sat back with a smile.

During photoshoots, many can put on a pretty or handsome smile. Suzanne was one of these individuals. The flip side is that there are times when a picture doesn't capture a "3-2-1 smile then shoot" image, but what is captured is a moment of authentic love and freedom. These moments cannot and will not ever be reproduced in a posed shot for the camera. What I saw was laughter and joy, and someone who wasn't caught up in the photoshoot itself. She was caught up in those who were her world and in a moment they would create, which just so happened to be captured in time.

To be honest, I don't remember the details of the rest of the visit. But I know that it had more laughter and fewer tears than years prior. It was an experience I'd prayed for for many years. It was a moment in which I was reminded that I was her son as well, and I was a reminder of the young man she had loved most in her life. Now George had reaped the rewards of standing by her side for so many years of struggle, pain, and suffering. I had and have nothing but total respect for him as a man of his word.

***

After replaying the prior years in my mind, I was brought back to the present as I drove down Cedar Hill toward the hospital. My heart began aching for them once again. "Can't these two catch a break?" I thought to myself.

Finally, I pulled into the parking lot of the hospital I knew all too well. I've spent several nights there, with my Uncle Andy and the last night my grandmother had lived as well as several long days with my dad. "Here we go again, Eddie. You know the drill."

After preparing myself, I walked into the hospital to find George. After hugging it out outside the ICU doors, which were far too familiar, we sat in the hallway to talk. After a short update, he asked "Are you ready to go see her?"

"Yes, I want to see her!"

As we walked through the doors, he led me down a familiar

hallway. I began smiling as we passed the nurses' station. "She's not alone," I thought to myself. I knew what room he was leading me to.

The rooms had four numbers. I knew the final two numbers. I believe the first two numbers were 10, but the final two were 12, the number both my brother and I had worn for our school's first and second football state championship. "Dad is in there with her," I told myself, as we walked into the room from which my dad left this world.

"This was my dad's room, George," I shared as we walked into the room.

"Really?" he looked at me, realizing what some might call a coincidence. "I'll leave you two alone. I'm gonna head outside to get some air."

Sitting in the room alone with her, I began talking to her. I spoke out to my dad as if he were in the room with us as well. "Dad, let her know it's going to be alright," I said to him, as if he were waiting on my direction.

While sitting with her, I got caught up in mixed emotions. This couldn't be happening because she'd finally found happiness in life. The all-too-common thought of "She doesn't deserve this, nor does George or Kelsey Morgan" filled my mind and heart.

Then the pounding of guilt hit me as I thought about this book, which should have been finished some time ago. "Did I let her down?" I asked myself as she lay before me. "No," I replied to myself. "Eddie, she didn't need the book, she just needed you." To this day, there are parts of me that still worry that I let her down, but then I remind myself of the relationship between us.

This woman told me several times that she loved me, always reminding me that I was her son as well. This beautiful, strong woman had raised a young man on her own until, later in life, God blessed her with George. She had a beautiful granddaughter who she taught how to be a young lady. Suzanne had a respect for the finer things in life and loved sharing them with Kelsey Morgan. She had lived a life of love, pain, struggle, and guilt, and as she laid before me, I found comfort in knowing that she no longer held onto the guilt of Robert's death. To me, that held the most importance.

After I'd had time with my other mom, George came back into the room. We sat in silence as the impact of what happened and was going to happen was unnerving.

"George, I never finished the book," I said, holding my head down in shame.

"Eddie, she'll know when it's done." He tried to help me release the guilt which began consuming me. The guilt I helped her release was the same guilt that was beginning to take hold of my heart. The fears of letting others down, which is, for many of us, the opening for acid to begin to enter and eat us internally.

I'd love to tell you that something more magical happened from here, but the remainder of that day is a blur. I didn't know this would be the last time I'd see her. Her sister had come into town and wanted to restrict visitors to family members as Suzanne was let go. I fully respected this choice.

I'd had my time and conversations with this beautiful woman. She was about to be reunited with Robert, and I took great comfort in knowing she would leave this world without any guilt from the choice her son had made. A warm feeling overtook me, knowing that my dad was there to lead her to her son given the importance Robert and Suzanne had in my life.

Amidst the hurt, pain, and suffering, there can be a beauty in this thing we call life. It was through being a part of the powerful moments of crying and questioning that some feelings were slowly released, and once they're released we can fill that void with something else. Mom chose to finally fill that void with forgiveness rather than another form of guilt. She forgave herself as well as her son, and that's where the magic lied.

The feelings of pain after losing someone shows the love that we have for that person. We would certainly do anything in the world for that person, even if it meant trading places. The question is, "If we have that love for someone else, why can't we love ourselves in the same manner?" This is a question you may want to ponder.

In the movie *Never Back Down*, there is a powerful conversation that takes place between two of the main characters. The conversation applies to us all.

"Sometimes, fighting the fight means you have to do the one thing you don't want to do. You have to fight for forgiveness! Everyone's got a fight!"

What are you fighting for? Forgiveness? Peace? The ability to move forward? To love? To love yourself? To free yourself from guilt and shame?

Begin fighting, and you'll find that you don't have power only when you reach the pinnacle of your destination. You'll step into your power the moment you decide to take action by taking control of your life.

Another powerful line from *Never Back Down* is, "Control the outcome, it's on you!"

Simply take one step forward.

TWELVE

It's important that we talk about this epidemic. One will learn to arm themselves and their loved ones with the proper weapons to battle this dilemma just by talking about it and bringing it out into the open.

How important is it that we talk about this epidemic of suicide? Is it a topic we should tip-toe around in hopes of it going away and not further impacting the lives of those left behind? Also, should we not bring this topic out into the open for those battling depression or thoughts of suicide? Will the topic of suicide trigger one to follow through with taking their own life?

A few years back I read *The Shack* by William P. Young, several years before the movie came out. The book had been recommended to me by a couple of friends, and it left me in tears and had a huge impact on me. It dove deep into my heart and brought to light some never-before-explored insights. When the movie was due to come out, I was excited. I hoped it would mirror the book as closely as possible. What I witnessed as the movie was released, however, as well as many of the comments I read disturbed me and pissed me off.

Read this word carefully: *fiction*. The definition of fiction is, "literature in the form of prose, especially short stories and novels, that describes imaginary events and people."

After this movie came out, many "Christians" criticized it for the ways the characters were portrayed in relation to the Bible. They shared the ways they felt it was a disgrace. The movie in no way portrayed what the Bible has signified throughout time. The comments that were being put out there left me with a bad taste in my mouth. It was a fictional movie, based on a fictional book!

After seeing the movie with my girlfriend, it brought a great deal of perspective to an important and sad time in her life. A friend of mine who was spending time in jail read the book, and it inspired him to focus on the importance of his life and allowed him to tap into a relationship with God. Another friend's mother passed the book on to him since he had endured a tragic accident at a young age, which not only impacted him but also his mother and father in a way I've never been able to fathom. Despite this fictional book and movie having been based upon imaginary events and people, it positively impacted the lives of a few people who are close to me. What if I told you that this story had brought some closer to God, while those who claim to be servants of God and others continue to bitch and judge? By the way, I do consider myself a Christian as a follower of the Bible.

This point isn't whether or not the book or movie is a legitimate representation of The Bible. It's simply a prime example of what a topic, movie, or book can do for others who need to hear a story, whether fiction or nonfiction.

The reason I share the controversy surrounding *The Shack* is that, regardless of the good trying to be shared in order to positively impact the lives of others, there are many who will attempt to downgrade or attack the works of one. There are many who attempt to discredit the works or actions of one in an attempt to place themselves above others. For those of you attempting to share your message in the most positive and influential manner, please don't stop, especially if you are coming from a place of love and healing.

When it comes to the topic of suicide, are there any solutions or tools one can arm themselves with? Is there an answer or magical solution that one can apply to fill their life with light and little to no darkness?

There isn't. There isn't just "one thing" we can implement in order to create one ideal solution for the variety of individuals in today's world. But, I want to share what I've implemented into my own life in order to never again get to a place where I'm contemplating my own existence and taking the action to end it all.

The first tool in my arsenal is fitness. Working out brings me life. The gym is a perfect place for me to gain a sense of power and strength, as it jolts me into releasing life's stresses and anxieties. More important than being inside the gym is being able to exercise outdoors through running, walking, or even hiking. I'm releasing the tension, improving my health, and enjoying the benefits of the sunlight and outdoors while feeling blessed by the gifts God has given us. Oh, and the side effects: improved cardio, an oxygenated body, and feeling good about the transformation of my body are wonderful.

The second thing I focus on pertains to fitness, in a way, but more so my health. I focus on alkalizing my body. Our body is naturally acidic in nature, and the counterbalance to acid is alkalinity. When I think of an acidic or an alkalized body, I think of these things:

- An alkalized body is an energized body.
- Acid eats away the negative charges surrounding our red blood cells, and if our pH balance is not above acidic, the red blood cells begin to clump

together, which in turn affects the oxygen flow to our brains.
- The body will store acid in our body fat to protect the acid in our blood from eating through the arterial walls.
- A highly acidic body creates more cholesterol to protect the arterial walls from the acid.

Do some of these facts sound important? It is important for the brain to have oxygen, isn't it? Also, are you able to best handle the stresses of life in an acidic state where you're feeling sluggish and low energy while experiencing cloudy thinking? Or, would you be better able to handle the tougher aspects of life when in an alkaline state, where your thinking is clearer and your body is healthier?

I'll leave it up to you to answer for yourself, but you can help yourself by monitoring the foods you eat. I'll share a list of foods that are alkaline in nature as well as a list of foods that are acidic in nature on my website, www.mindsetmtn.com. To be honest, and to give credit where credit is due, I learned a great deal about alkalinity through Tony Robbins and his course, "Get The Edge." He never referenced an acidic body tying into depression or suicide, but I took what he shared and dove a little deeper into how it might affect one battling depression.

The next thing I've implemented into my life is the Bible. For me, this is important, as I've found too many times in my life that there have been incidents that are more than coincidence. For you, it could simply be meditation or otherwise tapping into something beyond yourself. Remember, these are only *my* truths and actions, so take from them what you believe might benefit *you*. It could simply be walks in nature that bring about the same amount of peace and purpose.

Another release for me is reading. Reading takes me away from who I am and what I've been conditioned by throughout my life, and opens up possibilities of other ways to look at life.

Good stories such as *The Alchemist*, *The Greatest Salesman In The World*, or one of my favorites, *The Choice*, are stories that bring perspective and light to me.

Personal development books are powerful as well. The concepts in these books don't have to represent your truths completely, but if you can pull one aspect from each book you read and apply it to your personal life, how drastic could life change for you (for the better) over time?

There is one piece I pulled from the book *The Slight Edge* that holds a great deal of power for me, and it will apply to you as you attempt to move forward: *"What is easy to do, is also easy not to do!"* I have just given you several examples of steps you can take to improve your health, mind, and possibly soul. The question is: "Can you or will you willingly put in the effort to do the simple things that I've suggested?"

Can you and will you commit to reading 10 pages of a book every day for the next week, the next 90 days, or even the next 365 days?

Can you and will you willingly put in the effort to work out for 10-30 minutes, five days per week?

Can you and will you cut back on coffee or soda and add more lemon water or superfood green drinks to alkalize your body?

The last action I implemented into my life is journaling. To write down my thoughts and emotions or even share my thoughts about something I've read is a practice that helps me release those thoughts and emotions. What many fear about journaling their thoughts is the fear of what actually may lie in their thoughts. To journal is to be left alone with your thoughts, and not knowing exactly what those thoughts are can be scary. The truth is, you're alone with your thoughts anyway, so you might as well release them through pen and paper. To release them by typing them on a computer helps as well, but to sit in silence with a pen holds more power in my experience. Remember, "What's easy to do, is also easy not to do!" And yes,

I too fall off the wagon when it comes to doing the simple things. What's important is to immediately get your ass back up and jump back on that wagon.

If you're like I was for many years, you might come up with excuses as to why you can't read, journal, or exercise. You may have an hour commute to work or school, which is a perfect time to listen to podcasts. You may not have the money to join a gym or hire a fitness coach, but I'm willing to bet that you have access to YouTube for workouts or trails and places you can walk. Don't forget about pushups, sit-ups, or even burpees and planks, which you can easily add to your morning routine.

Are books too expensive? What about Goodwill, Bookmans, or even Savers or other second-hand stores? I just purchased two books at Goodwill by Tony Robbins and Stephen Covey at a total cost of $2.15 a few days ago. The message is, rather than looking for excuses as to *why you can't*, it's time to dive into a search for *how you can*!

I want to share a quick story with you that took place when my kids were younger.

My son and daughter were jumping off of my daughter's bed, which sat 4-5 feet off the ground. They were jumping onto a pile of blankets, having fun. While they were doing this, I was making my son's bed. Seeing that there was a possibility of them getting hurt, I told them if they got hurt and I heard crying, they might get a smack on the butt. They kept jumping.

Then it got silent.

"Bubs, are you okay?" I heard my daughter whisper.

I waited, but didn't turn around to see what had happened. I wanted to wait and see what was about to transpire. Finally, I turned around and saw my son with his hand over his eye. "Are you alright?" I asked. He nodded, not crying at all. He had hit his head on the rim of a trash can. I asked him to remove his hand, only to see a huge gash over his eye, straight through his eyebrow. I knew he definitely needed stitches.

We got to urgent care, and he still hadn't shed a tear. We saw the doctor, and after cleaning the gash, he began jabbing around the wound with a needle in order to numb it. Watching my son go through this, I wanted to hit the doctor! He gave me a look that said, "C'mon, Dad. This shit hurts"! Having watched my son hold it in as long as he could, I gave him permission to let out his emotions. I told him to go ahead and let it out, allowing him to go ahead and cry.

As we headed home, I shared with him that I was proud of him for toughing it out. My point wasn't that it isn't okay to cry; it was that there are times when we *feel* weaker than we actually are. I shared with him that any time he gets hurt, and it's less than a gash over the eye, there is no need to panic or lose control.

Through reading this book, it is my hope that you have no more excuses for not taking one small step toward the path of healing. There is hopefully no legitimate reason you are unable to read 10 pages a day, go for a walk, journal, or say No to junk food. Changes won't happen overnight. They take time. You are an empty cup that needs to be filled, but you sit right under the faucet as it drips, even at what feels like the slowest of rates. One drop adds next to nothing. Two drops doesn't add much more. Three drops make you wonder if the cup will *ever* fill. I need you to remember one thing: each drop is important. Without the first and second drop, you'll never fill your cup to overflowing. Without taking or adding small steps to your life to grow and heal, you will never get to the point of filling up and overflowing with love and happiness.

The flip-side to this is one I recently communicated to those who attended my cousin's funeral through the eulogy. The message was directed toward my cousins and those who were hurting. Several times, I saw individuals on social media telling my cousin's boys to "stay strong." So not only did I directly share this message with one of my cousins (second cousins), I shared it with everyone.

Don't stay strong!

Through staying strong long-term, we build up a wall to protect ourselves from pain and hurt. Through staying strong, we emotionally numb ourselves from pain and suffering. In the process, however, we also numb ourselves from the good in life. It's not an either/or switch we can flip.

If you're hurting emotionally, cry!

If you're hurting from life's battles, the loss of life, or even in search of your life's purpose, don't fear falling to your knees.

By staying strong, we sedate. We sedate through drugs, alcohol, and even sex. Money, business, and exercise become our tools of sedation to escape the issues of our lives. Sedation is sedation. The lesson we have to learn and face is how to go through our "go-throughs!" We have to allow ourselves to fall in order to realize the blessings of getting back up.

There are many yins and yangs to life.

Where there is the Devil, there is God.

Where there is black, there is white.

Where there is darkness, there is light.

Where there is sorrow, there is joy.

Where there is pain, there is healing.

Most important, where there is death, we have been given the gift and blessing of this thing called life!

THIRTEEN

As I wrap up this book, there is an important lesson I want to share—one which I learned and then shared with a loved one during a very important time in my life.

It is November 4, 2018. I have just pulled myself out of a little funk that I recently fell into for various reasons, the biggest of which was having lost a cousin due to a health failure. He was just a year older than I am.

At this time last year, I had lost an uncle to cancer four months prior. He was my dad's younger brother. Further, my mom was about endure one of the most emotionally trying times of her life to date.

In November 2017, my mom's husband was in the final month of his life. He had already battled cancer for two years. The time was near, as his cancer had spread and he had a choice to continue fighting or submit to the inevitable. My mom and her husband had been through a great deal over those past two years, but had so much to look back upon.

I chose to stay away as the time to say goodbye grew near, and he began closing doors to family and friends. He let those close to him know that the visit would be their last. He took the initiative to let them know of their importance in his life, but also that the next time he'd see them would be on the other side. I felt it was important for my mom and his son to go through this time together. My baby brother had come in from California to be with his dad, as his dad had asked him to stay till the end.

As frustration on the part of my mom and brother began to grow given the projected timeline—yet seeing no sign of him letting go—I decided to head to my mom's house to help out. They were becoming exhausted and began getting sick due to the emotional stress of keeping track of giving him his medication every two hours. My younger brother needed to get out of the house and find some sense of life outside the house in which his father had resided for some time.

Working our way through a Thanksgiving during which the highlight was the fact that this man's Minnesota Vikings won, I rejoiced in the knowledge that he was given another small victory as his days neared their end.

The Friday after Thanksgiving, pulling myself back from the situation, I began seeing something I couldn't fathom going through.

My mom, my brother, and I had given my step-dad the necessary drugs every two hours to keep his pain at a minimum. He had said his final goodbyes to everyone important to him. So what was holding him back from truly committing to let go?

Then it hit me.

Each time his son walked out of the room created a time during which he'd have to commit to letting go and being at peace with the fact that that moment would be the last time he'd see his son on this side of Heaven. This would be one door that he was not be able to close, which is why he continued to fight.

After having brought this up to my mom, we had a talk with my brother. It was hard for all of us, especially the young man who didn't want his father to leave, but wanted him to finally be at peace.

We had to take the decision out of the hands of his father; we agreed that we had to make the decision for him. My brother had to make the decision and be at peace with it. He left the Saturday morning after Thanksgiving, leaving his father with myself and his mother. He said his goodbyes, lifting the weight off of his dad's shoulders. This was hard to witness. My baby brother had to find peace in leaving his dad so the man who raised him could peacefully let go.

Then the shift began.

On Saturday night, as my mom was becoming even more sick, I tended to this amazing man every two hours. During the night, he continued calling on me for this or that, and asked several things of me. He was thirsty, and wanted water. He wanted me to unplug the clock, as he could sense the energy from the light and the electronics. I'd walk out of the room, only to be called back in to unplug the diffuser from which he could feel the energy and sense the purple light reflecting in the closet door mirror. In hindsight, it's funny, but it began to become frustrating at the time…until I realized what it was that he was doing.

"I need you to let your mom know her work is done and let her know not to come in here any more," he told me.

"Got it," I responded. "I'll let her know."

That was the final door he had to close. It was sad and painful to let her know, but she knew exactly what was going on. And I knew what was going on.

The morning came, and he was still rocking and rolling. He wanted to get up to use the restroom for the final time. Boy, this man was a handful! But, as I threatened to bring my mom back to the room if he didn't chill out, what I didn't know was that he was preparing himself for one final act of courage, one that exemplified the type of man he was.

After getting him back in bed, he commanded, "Send your mom in here."

Hearing these words brought me a major sense of peace and

respect for him. He stepped up to his final promise to love and cherish this woman as his wife of over 26 years.

"Eddie's got it from here," he let her know as she walked in. There was more to be said, which was nothing short of beautiful, but that is a moment I'll leave between them.

He was ready to let go as he closed that final door. At least that was my hope.

After going in several more times to give him his medication, I had asked him if he wanted me to darken the room. It was daytime, and I realized that the light coming in from the window might be a distraction.

"I'll go get some sheets to hang over the window," I told him, as I prepared to walk out of the room.

"No, get aluminum foil," he responded.

"We're all out, I just used up the last of it," I said.

"Then send your mom to the store to get more," he commanded.

In that moment, I realized what he was truly trying to do. I became agitated and upset. We were all exhausted.

"No. I'm not going to send her to the store," I told him. "She's not feeling good, and she's done a great deal for you."

At first I felt bad, but I then had to find a way to get through to him.

"I know what you're doing. You're trying to control this whole situation. You want everything in place the way *you* want it. You want this to go the way *you* want it to go! Here's the deal," I shared. "You have two choices. One is to try to control this whole situation, and in turn the control will eventually be taken away from you, which won't happen the way you want it to happen. The second option is to release the control, which will allow you to have final control. You can have final control by releasing control. It will be a beautiful journey home. Or, the choice for that kind of journey can be taken away from you, which is something I don't want for you. You choose." Then I walked out to the living room where my mom was.

After having shared this exchange with her, she began growing agitated. Mind you, she was exhausted as hell, not to mention sick. "You tell him I'll go in there if he doesn't chill out," she said, as we both chuckled with a hint of seriousness. The way it was going, he would outlive both of us! I even joked that we'd wheel him into his own memorial party if he chose not to let go, which I'd scheduled a few weeks out.

"Eddie!" we heard coming from the bedroom. My mom and I looked at each other.

"I got this," I told her, wanting her to relax.

As I walked through the door to the bedroom, asking what he needed, he responded, "You're right, I'm sorry."

You want to talk about feeling like shit? I felt horrible. Then again, I didn't.

"I want this to be a beautiful journey for you, as it should be. I love you. You're important to me, my brothers, my kids, and most importantly, my mom. It's time for you to go home."

"Ok," he responded, grasping the importance of my words.

"I love you. I always will," I said before walking out the door.

Within the next two hours, he slipped into a coma and never again woke as he slowly worked his way home. Monday passed, and by Tuesday, I knew it was safe enough for my mom to visit with her husband again. I needed short reprieve, so my mom jumped back in to help for a few hours. I walked in to the bedroom with my mom and Jack, this man's dearest friend, who'd stood by his side day-in and day-out. Jack was a rescue dog who became his companion and protector as he battled his illness. Jack jumped up on the bed and gave his dad kisses before he headed home. They had their final goodbye.

On Wednesday, my other younger brother needed a ride home after locking his keys in his truck. As we left, my mom jumped on the phone with my baby brother. As she sat on the edge of the bed talking with her youngest son, there in this house, in this room, was the presence of a man and his wife, along with that of their son.

Walking into the house immediately after their phone call ended, I walked in to give him his medication. His journey on Earth had ended. He finally arrived home.

***

There are many times in life when we want to control everything. We want to line things up the way we want them to be lined up, not the way they should be lined up. Yes, it would be great if our lives went according to our own plans. If this were the case, however, I can almost guarantee that you wouldn't have experienced some of the blessings in life that you have.

Some of my biggest blessings have come from what I felt during the darkest of times. During these times, however, I believed I might have made my biggest mistakes. My marriage didn't work out—but if if weren't for my marriage, I wouldn't have had my son who is now 16, or my 19-year-old daughter who I began raising when she was just a year and a half old, always loving her as my own.

The day my dad went into the hospital and the manner in which it happened wasn't ideal, but the last conversation we had was about a passion we had together: coaching and baseball.

Sometimes we just have to accept that which has been given. We have to be grateful for the experiences and lessons that are taught and learned. We may find that the path we *want* to travel may not be right for us, but the path we keep getting redirected toward is the one that *is* meant to be, for us and for others. At no point in my life did I decide that I've wanted to grow up and write a book on the impacts of suicide. But when I write, it is easiest for me to tap into my emotions, which I consider a gift from God.

This book is based upon *my* truths; it's as simple as that. This is *my* story based upon *my* experiences and the way I see those experiences. To relinquish control and allow myself to be led has brought me to the completion of this book.

I've tried for years, in various ways, to control this whole thing called life. In doing so, I became a man full of bullshit stories and lies. I became a man of false commitments to self and others. I felt I was in control and on the path to greatness—as long as it went the way I wanted it to go. This approach led to a snowball of lies. Most importantly, I began failing in so many ways that I didn't know which way was up.

At no time will I tell you that I am one hundred percent dialed in to this thing called life. But I *will* tell you that, once I began controlling certain aspects of my life that I can and should attempt to control, I began getting positive results.

Life is and will always be a rollercoaster, full of ups and downs. It will hit us from behind, and sometimes upside the head. But the truth is, in the end, as the sun sets, it can and will be a beautiful journey if we allow it to be.

At times we will have to get back up. And we can.

Other times, we will have to help others get back up. And we can.

At times we will have to release control by trusting and growing in patience. And we can.

Other times, we will have to take control in how we respond and how we choose to react. And we can.

As I shared early on, "If you ride the rollercoaster and say it's the funnest ride ever invented, and then I ride it, sharing it's the scariest thing on earth, who is right?" Our lives are based upon perspectives, and the way I see things may or may not be true for you. Shoot, your truths may or may not be true to me, but that's the beauty of life, isn't it? It's about the journey. It's about growth. It's about so much more than we realize, but this is only the case if you choose to see at as such.

I pray that you find the beauty in your life, no matter the pitfalls and struggles you've encountered or will encounter. You will have a choice to declare life the worst experience ever created for mankind, or you can be grateful and find the beauty in it. Though today you may encounter the worst of circumstances, remember to fight one more day. Remember that your todays don't have to define your tomorrows. Take control of what you do today, realizing the results may not be exactly what you want…yet!

Keep learning.
Keep growing.
Keep serving.
Keep fighting.

ACKNOWLEDGMENTS

To Makynzie and Andres, forever my loves. Watching you becoming the young woman and man you are molding yourselves into, I could not be any more proud of the impacts you will have upon this world. I have been, and always will be, your proud father.

To Jodi Michelle, Your continued support to me and the book is proof of the commitment you've made to us! This book has created a great deal of stress for us both, and you've always seen the possibilities to impact lives that would come from its completion. Thank you for pushing me to get this book out to those in need. I'm grateful to God for your love, despite my faults and the tough times we've gone through. I love you!

To Kelsey Morgan, I know this book will release a range of emotions for you. Through them, however, I pray you find peace, knowing that the place of love you held in your dad's heart never left him. I know this because as a father, I too hit that point! I love you, young lady, and you will always hold a place in my heart.

To my Uncle Teddy, your continuous support and love have always shed light upon my life. I cannot thank you enough for always having belief in me. And for you, Aunt Liz, words can't express how you always having my back has brought comfort to me in knowing I'm never alone.

To Jason "J-Boom" Legaard, my brother from another mother, your continuous support and insights have always stayed with me. You never once doubted the power of my story, even when I doubted it myself. Gratitude, my brother!

To Bill and Lyndsey Kuche, I will never be able to share how instrumental you two have been to me through the darkest of times in my life. By trusting me with your babies and by stepping up as Godparents to my daughter, you two will forever hold a place in my heart.

To Phillip and Jen Guirlanda as well as Mike and Lori Langan, the support you four have brought me during tough times will never be able to be repaid. Thank you for including me in your families.

To Silas Page, I will never be able to say "Thank you" enough, not just for employing me, but even more for allowing me to be a father in the lives of my children.

To Cindy Quinley, Jason Legaard, Lyndy Pearson, Darleen Payne, and Leann Pearson Capener, along with six other individuals (anonymous) who believed in the purpose of this book some time ago, thank you for supporting me in this vision. It took some time, but it's complete.

To Bill Sutton, your support and trust in me has etched its way into the foundation I pray to sustain from this day forward. You are a man amongst men, forever impacting the lives of others.

To Linda Sutton, your warm heart and compassion will forever touch me. I will never be able to tell you how honored I am that you trusted me enough to share your story. Thank you!

To Jerry Payne, I will forever consider you a brother. The courage it took for you to share a part of yourself will definitely impact others. Spuck would be proud, my brother.

To Jeff Otero, we have been and always will be family. From

our times as little kids to growing up as men with our own families, may our truths bring perspective to the lives of others. I love you, my brother.

This last acknowledgment is one that I will forever hold dear. This book has been a vision. This book has frightened me. This book has been something that I've given up on many times. Elizabeth Lyons, thank you for bringing this book to fruition. Words can't describe how it's felt to trust you to take what I've seen and felt in my heart and translate it into this book. Thank You!

ABOUT THE AUTHOR

Edward Aguilar is the father of two amazing children, an inspirational speaker, and a cerebral strategist. He explores what others have accomplished, identifies the pivotal moments they may not have seen as important, and uses them as the basis to create a solid foundation to begin rebuilding the *real* person that the world needs to see.

For twelve years, he fought wild fires, and spent ten of those years as a Hotshot firefighter. From working on mindset to beliefs and attitudes toward life, self-image, and events to realizing the importance of one's physical activity and diet and its effect on one's overall well-being.

He's also "just human." He's gone through both divorce and foreclosure and almost gave up on life after a close friend took his own life.

He believes that in life, the struggle to find balance brings about turmoil at times. He's led in many circumstances in life, but what made the difference was knowing that a good leader must also be a good student.

It's time for you to rebuild. And if you've read this far, this book was meant to find its way into your hands.

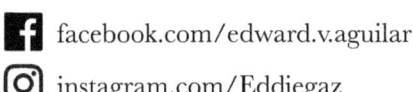

facebook.com/edward.v.aguilar

instagram.com/Eddiegaz

www.ingramcontent.com/pod-product-compliance
Lightning Source LLC
Chambersburg PA
CBHW051655040426
42446CB00009B/1143